DIDACHE

Early Christian Apocrypha

Julian V. Hills

Harold W. Attridge

Dennis R. Macdonald

VOLUME 1: *THE ACTS OF ANDREW*

VOLUME 2: *THE EPISTLE OF THE APOSTLES*

VOLUME 3: *THE ACTS OF THOMAS*

VOLUME 4: *THE ACTS OF PETER*

VOLUME 5: *DIDACHE*

DIDACHE

THE TEACHING OF
THE TWELVE APOSTLES

CLAYTON N. JEFFORD

Cover and interior design by Robaire Ream

Library of Congress Cataloging-in-Publication Data

Didache. English
 Didache = The teaching of the twelve apostles / [translation and notes by Clayton
N. Jefford]. -- First [edition].
     p. cm. -- (Early Christian Apocrypha ; 5)
 Includes bibliographical references and index.
 ISBN 978-1-59815-126-8 (alk. paper)
 1. Theology, Doctrinal--History--Early church, ca. 30-600--Early works to 1800. I.
Jefford, Clayton N., translator. II. Title. III. Title: Teaching of the twelve apostles.
 BS2940.T4A3 2013
 270.1--dc23
                                                                2013023765

CONTENTS

SIGLA, ABBREVIATIONS, CONVENTIONS

1,2 Clem	*1,2 Clement*
1 Cor	1 Corinthians
1,2 Kgs	1,2 Kings
1,2 Pet	1,2 Peter
1QS	*Rule of the Community*
1QSa	*Rule of the Congregation* (Appendix to 1QS)
1,2 Thess	1,2 Thessalonians
1 Tim	1 Timothy
1,2,3,4 Macc	1,2,3,4 Maccabees
ApCon	*Apostolic Constitutions* (7.1.2–32.4)
AposTrad	Hippolytus, *The Apostolic Tradition*
Arab	Arabic version (given in Greek)
Barn	*Epistle of Barnabas* (18.1–21.1)
CO	*Apostolic Church Order*
Col	Colossians
Copt	Coptic text of Did 10.3–12.2a
Deut	Deuteronomy
Did	*Didache*
Dida	*Didascalia apostolorum*
Doct	*Doctrina apostolorum* (Latin text of *Didache*?)
EcclHist	Eusebius, *Ecclesiastical History*
Eph	Ephesians
Epit	*Epitome of the Canons of the Holy Apostles*
Eth	Ethiopic text of Did 8.1–2a; 11.3–5, 7–12; 12.1–13.1, 3–7 (given in Greek)
Exod	Exodus
Gal	Galatians
Geor	Georgian text of *Didache* (given in Greek)
H	Greek text of *Didache* (Codex Hierosolymitanus)
HermMan	*Shepherd of Hermas, Mandate*
HermSim	*Shepherd of Hermas, Similitude*
HermVis	*Shepherd of Hermas, Vision*
IgnEph	Ignatius, *To the Ephesians*
IgnMag	Ignatius, *To the Magnesians*
IgnTr	Ignatius, *To the Trallians*

IgnPhd	Ignatius, *To the Philadelphians*
IgnSm	Ignatius, *To the Smyrnaeans*
Isa	Isaiah
Jas	James
Jer	Jeremiah
JusAp	Justin, *First Apology*
JusDia	Justin, *Dialogue with Trypho*
Lev	Leviticus
Mal	Malachi
Matt	Matthew
Neh	Nehemiah
NT	New Testament
Pet	*Gospel of Peter*
Phil	Philippians
POxy	Oxyrhynchus Papyrus
Prov	Proverbs
Ps(s)	Psalm(s)
Rev	Revelation
Rom	Romans
Sir	Sirach
Strom	Clement of Alexandria, *Stromata*
TAsh	Testament of Asher
TDan	Testament of Dan
TGad	Testament of Gad
Thom	Gospel of Thomas
TIss	Testament of Issachar
TJud	Testament of Judah
TLevi	Testament of Levi
Tob	Tobit
Wis	Wisdom of Solomon
Zech	Zechariah
<and>	words supplied *ad sensum*
[then]	words supplied as emendation
. . .	words deliberately omitted
columns	where both versions survive, the Greek text of H is presented on the left side, the texts of POxy 1782, Doct, and Copt on the right
†	see the Additional Note, after the main translation

INTRODUCTION

Philotheos Bryennios (1833–1914/18) rediscovered the *Didache*, or *Teaching of the Twelve Apostles*, in the Greek Orthodox metropolitan of Nicomedia in 1873. Its publication a decade later caused an immediate sensation. Theologians and historians of ecclesiastical literature offered excited conjectures about the importance of the text for the foundations of the faith, its ability to provide access to the ancient mindset, and its potential to unlock mysteries about the first generation of Christians beyond the authors of the New Testament (NT). A number of commentaries soon appeared, including works by such scholars as Adolf Hilgenfeld (1884), Adolf von Harnack (1884), Paul Sabatier (1885), R. D. Hitchcock and Francis Brown (1885), Philip Schaff (1885), and Charles Taylor (1886). A variety of journal articles and monograph studies accompanied these volumes and spawned a general recognition that the text was something of a "riddle" (Vokes 1938) or "enigma" (Giet 1970), with respect to both its construction and theology.

Examination of the text has led scholarship along various avenues of investigation since that time. Ample material exists to explore the foundational elements of ancient Christian tradition, particularly as intertwined with Jewish motifs and traditions. Elements of the teachings of Jesus and his earliest followers appear throughout. Parallels with the gospels predominate, especially with respect to the trajectory of Matthew. The text features a variety of liturgical instructions—most notably with reference to baptism, prayer, and eucharist—along with directives on the organization of the early community. Such materials and regulations have led many scholars to identify the *Didache* as a "handbook" or "ecclesiastical manual" in use early in the evolution of Christianity's development of early church orders, though this concept has received considerable debate in recent decades and remains to be settled (Mueller 2007, 337–80).

The structure of the *Didache* is easily determined, even if its transitional elements remain only roughly apparent (Pardee 2012). In a basic sense the work features four primary divisions:

Chaps. 1–6: The *Didache* opens with the classic theme of the "two ways" of existence known from both Jewish literature and Greek philosophy. The first of these ways—the way of life—is explained in great detail over the course of chapters 1–4 using the Decalogue as the essential framework of instruction. The Didachist (that is, the original author of the text) supplemented warnings

1

against murder, adultery, theft, etc., with additional counsel against numer-ous other human failings, such as arrogance, hypocrisy, jealousy, and the use of magic. The materials reflect two primary avenues of approach: a classical pattern of instruction that incorporates the phrase "my child" from Jewish wisdom literature, and a typically Jewish *fence* construction of lesser "sins" that the reader is counseled to shun in order to avoid the transgression of more meaningful offenses as defined by the Decalogue. A secondary segment (known as the "ecclesiastical section") may be included here at 1.3a–2.1, which a later editor likely inserted. The way of death is described in brief in chapter 5, offering a distillation of the central elements of the previous ma-terials as the road toward certain destruction. Finally, the section closes with warnings to avoid those who teach without regard for this tradition.

Chaps. 6–10 contain teachings about how the Christian is to conduct the daily affairs of a ritually appropriate life. There are four such, including teachings on which foods are appropriate to eat, how a proper baptism is to be conducted, the suitable days on which to fast, and fitting words by which to pray. These teachings begin at the end of chapter 6 (as the text has been divided by modern editors), perhaps suggesting a link between them and the previous instructions on the "two ways." Of particular interest is the almost verbatim repetition of the Lord's prayer, in the form known otherwise from Matt 6:9–13, as a standard for personal prayer. Beyond this prayer, however, are two sets of prayers to be said over the cup and bread when one "gives thanks." Some scholars suppose that these or similar prayers were said at the formal ritual of the eucharist (Jefford 1989, 140; LaVerdiere 1996, 138–45), but this remains a matter of dispute.

Chaps. 11–15: A series of directives follow the above. These relate to lead-ership and authority within the community. The first community "office" addressed is that of teachers and the nature of what they teach, somewhat reminiscent of chapter 6 above. Then come instructions on the reception of apostles and prophets into the community. Such persons required special attention, especially the latter, since it would have been both difficult and dangerous to "judge the Spirit" as one evaluated a potential prophet, a task that was awkward for the leaders of any worshipping community. A large portion of this section is consumed with the process by which visitors may be evaluated, and strict guidelines by which to make the determination of "true prophets" who were worthy to live and serve among the readers. The sec-tion concludes with two additional instructions. The first of these relates to the appropriate nature by which believers may participate in the worship of the community and the acceptable frame of mind for offering sacrifices. The second speaks to how leaders (bishops and deacons) must be appointed and the respect that is due them. Finally, there is a general call for the faithful to act appropriately toward one another, offering acceptable corrections when necessary, repenting when expected, and leading lives of prayer and charity.

Chap. 16 is given over entirely to the matter of keeping faithful to the end of time and the expectation of a period of tribulation that will occur prior to the appearance of the "son of God." These words parallel materials in 1 Thessalonians and the gospels of Mark and Matthew (Balabanski 1997, 180–205). The tone is decidedly eschatological, somewhat reflective of that which appears in Revelation, and foreshadowed in the tenor of the eucharistic prayers of chapters 9–10 above. The appearance of such materials at the conclusion of the work is perhaps not unexpected. But apart from the eucharistic prayers, there is nothing else in the *Didache* to suggest such an orientation (Draper 2011). It is not entirely clear that today's readers still have the actual concluding words of the text preserved in the single manuscript that remains, which has led scholars to debate what other verses may have been lost to the tradition. In either case, there does not appear to be too much of the manuscript tradition lost from the conclusion.

A strong Matthean framework of thought undergirds the entire text of the *Didache*. Frequent parallels to Matthew appear throughout, some of these in the form of entire sayings and specific traditions, others in the guise of key words and phrases. The very theme of the "two ways" itself, for example, is only found explicitly in this form in the NT within Matthew (7:13–14). The same is true with respect to the observation in the beatitudes that the meek shall inherit the earth (5:5), the better known form of the Lord's prayer (6:9–13), and the use of the Trinitarian formula (28:19).

Scattered scriptural echoes touch on most of the remaining NT texts, including all the gospels, Acts, letters of Paul, Hebrews, James, 1 Peter, 1–2 John, Jude, and Revelation. These are much more limited in usage however. There is a clear emphasis on texts and teachings from the Hebrew scriptures as well, especially the Decalogue of Exodus and Deuteronomy, Numbers, Nehemiah, Psalms, Proverbs, Job, Isaiah, Jeremiah, Joel, Zechariah, and Malachi. Finally, several intertestamental writings find representation throughout—including Tobit, Wisdom of Solomon, 3 Maccabees, and the Testament of Gad—but most significant here are parallels drawn from Sirach, whose teachings come second in prominence only with respect to Matthew. There is no question that the Didachist was well informed about scriptural materials and the traditions that reflected them. This is perhaps the primary reason that scholars have found the text so intriguing for over a century.

While it is evident that the *Didache* fell within a developing tradition of textual interpretation, it is also clear that various early ecclesiastical authors knew it and considered it to have authority. For example, many materials in Book 7 of the fourth-century *Apostolic Constitutions* are structured around the framework of the *Didache*, indicating that the compiler of that work was well aware of the text and felt it had value for instruction within the church. Eusebius of Caesarea listed it among the "disputed writings" (EcclHist 3.25.4–7), indicating that he was unsure of its authorship, though he acknowledged that it held the esteem of many theologians. Clement of Alexandria may even have considered the text to be "scripture" (γραφή), though his use of the term in this regard is disputed by scholars. He offers a few possible quotations from the *Didache*, yet these primarily reflect the "two ways" tradition alone and may have been taken from a tractate that featured this tradition as a separate literary work rather than the whole of the *Didache* (Niederwimmer 1998, 6–8).

Of particular interest within the *Didache* is the collection of liturgical traditions and ecclesiastical instructions that either are unique to the text or not found elsewhere in the literature prior to the appearance of the work. See especially the prayers of chapters 9–10, words of thanksgiving that have rough parallels to contemporary *berakah* blessings of the Jewish synagogue tradition, though not in the same exact form. The remaining question among scholars is whether these prayers are actually unique to the early Christian tradition (since they appear nowhere else) or are instead typical of ancient Christian liturgical practices in a form that has been superseded by subsequent usage.

As for ecclesiastical instructions, the *Didache* is the earliest known document outside the NT to identify the problem of settled faith communities in conflict with traveling, itinerant preachers and prophets. The Didachist does not doubt the validity of such persons, but recognizes that not all of them are worthy witnesses to the teachings of Jesus of Nazareth. Those who preach falsely for their own gain are identified as "Christ peddlers" (χριστέμπορος; 12.5), a term known first from the *Didache*. The difficulty with such persons is the complexity of their identification. When the community *accepts* a "Christ peddler" into its midst, it risks the newcomer becoming truly destructive to the good of the unity of the church. The danger that results from *rejecting* a worthy prophet, however, is likewise problematic in terms of snubbing the power of the Spirit to do divine work within the world. Such struggles reflect the nature of early Christian community formation during the late first and early second centuries, an evolution that finds no greater witness than in the text of the *Didache*.

An especially intriguing aspect of the text is the author's (and hence presumably the community's) close association with Jewish tradition. A previous generation of scholars quickly assumed that such links placed the work as a mid-second–century (or later) writing that had survived in a unique backwater of early Christian development. As such, it was believed to represent an earlier form of the faith that eventually grew stagnant and finally disappeared as the church moved from its original Jewish roots to a broader non-Jewish audience. More recent studies have suggested another scenario however. It now seems much more likely that the text reflects an especially early form of the faith—perhaps with roots that even precede the work of the apostle Paul—that was commonly known and respected around the Mediterranean world of the first century (Milavec 2003; Garrow 2004). The specifics of such a faith are not entirely clear, but their association with the synagogue seems evident from the Jewish nature of the teachings that remain, the prayers that are spoken, and the view of community that reflects a structure familiar from rabbinic literature.

Consider the theology the Didachist offers throughout the construction of the text. Unlike the preaching of Paul and the subsequent narrative of the NT gospels, the *Didache* contains no focus on the cross and resurrection of Jesus of Nazareth. In this respect the author exhibits a rather "low christology" that finds no parallel in comparison with the writings of the NT and subsequent authors such as Ignatius of Antioch and the *Epistle of Barnabas*. Nor is Jesus ever specifically given a designation of divinity within the text. He is simply called "servant, child" (παῖς) in the prayers and referenced as "the Lord" (ὁ κύριος) elsewhere. Readers are instructed "not [to] pray like the hypocrites but, as the Lord instructed in his gospel" (8.2). Elsewhere, the reference to not giving holy things to dogs is introduced with the words "for the Lord has also spoken about this" (9.5); and readers are directed to "offer your prayers and charity and all your actions just as you discern in the gospel of our Lord" (15.4). At the same time, a similar designation is given to God the Father, as when the author attributes quotations of Mal 1:11, 14 to "the Lord" (14.3). In certain respects one may find a cultural sensitivity at work in these usages, since they may be designed to offer the squeamish Christian Jew an opportunity to consider the divine nature of the messiah without risking a denial of the basic Jewish confession that "the Lord is our God, the Lord alone" (Deut 6:4). In other words, the text hints at the exalted nature of the messiah without explicitly demanding a confession that denies the essential tenets of traditional Jewish faith.

Similar theological tendencies appear throughout. The initial focus on the "two ways" bears nothing specifically Christian in its essence, since it occurs elsewhere in the Jewish and Greek literature of the first and second centuries. Instructions on eating, baptism, fasting, and prayer also do not defy traditional Jewish norms, though certain elements appear to push the boundaries of customary synagogue practices. For example, the reader is instructed to "accept what you can" (6.3) with respect to the selection of foods otherwise forbidden by laws of *kosher*. Likewise, the celebrant is to baptize "in the name of the Father and of the Son and of the Holy Spirit" (7.1, 3) as a sure sign of messianic expectation only otherwise explicitly identified in scripture at Matt 28:19. And the community is instructed neither to fast nor to pray "with the hypocrites" (8.1–2)—likely a reference to non-messianic Jews, as opposed to the "scribes and Pharisees" who served as opponents to Jesus in the NT gospels.

The only complete form of the *Didache* known from tradition appears in a single Greek manuscript from the eleventh century now housed in the Patriarchate at Jerusalem. Found in 1873 by Philotheos Bryennios among the manuscripts of the library of the Monastery of the Holy Sepulchre in Constantinople, the text (known variously as Codex Hierosolymitanus or the Jerusalem Codex, most often simply cited as "H") was published by Bryennios in 1883 and moved to Jerusalem in 1887.

The manuscript is included in a leather-bound, 120-page codex that features the following writings in order: *Synopsis of Holy Scripture* by Pseudo-Chrysostom, *Epistle of Barnabas, 1-2 Clement*, a list of the "books of the Hebrews," the *Didache*, a longer recension of the letters of Ignatius, and comments on the genealogy of Jesus. Bryennios first published *1-2 Clement* before recognizing the value of the *Didache* text. The manuscript is attributed to the scribe "Leon the notary and sinner," who claims to have completed the work on 11 June 1056 (col. 120a). The literary hand is careful and well-ordered. Mistakes of orthography are few and scattered, though corrections and clarifications appear throughout. Photographic plates are readily available (Harris 1887). A few terms are misspelled through the likely process of *iotacism* (a reduction of vowels and diphthongs toward the pronunciation of an iota sound), but the scribe himself appears to have caught most of these and has offered corrections above the line. It is not certain that the text of the *Didache* is complete here, since the manuscript leaves a space of some seven and a half lines before the next work in the collection, a tendency not otherwise typical of the scribe. The work ends with the phrase "coming on the clouds of the sky," words that receive expansion elsewhere in the manuscript tradition (Audet 1958, 73–74; Garrow 2004, 29–66).

H begins with two headings. The shorter title of "Teaching of the Twelve Apostles" appears as a superscription, with the longer label of "Teaching of the Lord to the Nations through the Twelve Apostles" written on the first line that follows. The words of the text begin on the same line. The shorter title likely was originally attached as an incipit in earlier forms of the tradition. No particular markings distinguish the movement between sections, though the scribe offers several superscript designs throughout whose meaning remains unclear.

Because this is the only extant manuscript that likely was written in the same language as the original, its value cannot be underestimated. Yet scholars often assume that mistakes and conjectural emendations permeate the text because it appeared so late in the process of transmission. Bryennios (1883) had already made a number of corrections based on such suppositions, followed in turn by Hilgenfeld (1884), von Harnack (1886), and others. But unfortunately there is little available in the history of the work to help with adjustments to the manuscript tradition apart from imaginative speculation based on the few fragmentary literary parallels that remain in other languages and in later traditions. As a result, the translation provided by most commentaries contains only minor adjustments and corrections to the Greek manuscript itself.

The only other text of the *Didache* that remains in Greek is a brief fragment now housed in the Ashmolean Museum of Art and Archaeology at the University of Oxford in England. Identified as Oxyrhynchus Papyrus 1782 (Grenfell and Hunt 1922, 12), this text appears to be a badly worn section of papyrus taken from a small fourth-century codex. Both sides of this fragment contain materials from what may have been a longer version of the *Didache*, the one side preserving 1.3c–1.4a of the text and the other containing 2.7b–3.2.

Despite its brevity, this fragment is highly significant for two primary reasons. Its origins in the fourth century make it some seven centuries older than H, roughly equivalent to the date of the *Apostolic Constitutions* (ApCon), whose author incorporated the *Didache* into Book 7 of that work. The text represented here is thus an earlier link in the tradition, though it is not clear that this fragment and H depend on the same manuscript lineage. In addition, the work preserves some wording from the so-called "ecclesiastical section" (1.3b–2.1a), suggesting that this segment was either original to the text or, more likely, an addition that occurred prior to the fourth century.

It remains unclear that either H or POxy 1782 is superior to the other as a witness to the exemplar of the *Didache*. Each bears features that are supported independently by other literature within the evolutionary history of the text.

LATIN

The Latin form of the *Didache*, known as the *Doctrina apostolorum* (Doct), is known from two medieval manuscripts: the ninth-century Mellicensis 597 (1.1–3a; 2.2–6 only) housed in the Stiftsbibliothek at Melk in Austria, and the eleventh-century Monacensis lat. 6264 (1.1–3a; 2.2–6.1) found in the Staatsbibliothek of Munich in Germany. The manuscripts diverge in only minor ways, which suggests they share a common archetype (van de Sandt and Flusser 2002, 113–20).

The Latin tradition unfortunately contains only roughly equivalent parallels to H at 1.1–6.1. Even here the materials of 1.2b–2.1a as found in the Greek are missing, yet another hint that perhaps these verses were not original to the text of H (Layton 1968, 343–83). The ending at 6.1 also differs from the Greek, again recommending that the author did not know the additional materials now preserved in H. Such an abrupt conclusion to the text indicates either that the Latin rendition reflects an independent witness to the ancient "two ways" tradition prior to its inclusion into the *Didache*, or that another tradition lies altogether separate from the evolution of the text. For present purposes it is included in the textual reconstruction below as a parallel to the manuscript of H, worthy for consideration in understanding the evolution of the textual tradition. It must be admitted that not all scholars agree with this opinion; some argue that it represents a different tradition of the "two ways" altogether or, at best, a homily fragment based on the *Didache* (Robinson 1920, 74; Connolly 1923, 154–55).

Several elements within Doct give further clarification by which to understand the text of the *Didache*. These are related primarily to inclusions and omissions against the textual tradition of H. One observes, for example,

Did 1.1

H   There are two ways—one of life and one of death (ὁδοὶ δύο εἰσί μία τῆς ζωῆς καὶ μία τοῦ θανάτου)

Doct There are two ways in the world—life and death, light and darkness. Two angels are placed over them—one over what is right, another over what is flawed (*viae duae sunt in saeculo, uitae et mortis, lucis et tenebrarum: in his constituti sunt angeli duo, unus aequitatis, alter iniquitatis*)

The presence of angelology in the Latin tradition finds ready parallel elsewhere in the literature (especially in *Hermas*, *Barnabas*, and at Qumran), but no such influence is evident in the *Didache*. The Didachist likewise does not include the concepts of "light and dark," preferring instead to focus on elements of ethical lifestyle and appropriate community standards. This suggests a specific mindset for the author that generally lies beyond elements of cosmic tone.

Did 2.7

H   Do not hate anyone—but reprimand some, pray for some—and some you shall love more than yourself (οὐ μισήσεις πάντα ἄνθρωπον, ἀλλὰ οὓς μὲν ἐλέγξεις, περὶ δὲ ὧν προσεύξῃ, οὓς δὲ ἀγαπήσεις ὑπὲρ τὴν ψυχήν σου)

Doct Do not hate anyone—some you shall love more than your soul (*neminem hominum oderis, quosdam amabis super animam tuam*)

The Greek phrasing "but reprimand some, pray for some"—which, much like the secondary materials of 1.3b–2.1, is also missing in Doct—suggests the influence of gospel traditions not original to the text. Thus, Matt 18:15's admonition "to correct (ἐλέγχω)" one another shows a clear influence on Did 15.3, as indicated by the phrase "as you have in the gospel." This wording likely reflects a later editorial hand already familiar with Matthew, which presumably is also revealed by the parallel phrase about reprimand and prayer now found in the Greek at 2.7.

Did 4.14

H   Disclose your wrongdoings in the community and do not approach your prayer with an evil conscience (ἐν ἐκκλησίᾳ ἐξομολογήσῃ τὰ παραπτώματά σου, καὶ οὐ προσελεύσῃ ἐπὶ προσευχήν σου ἐν συνειδήσει πονηρᾷ)

Doct   Do not approach prayer with an evil conscience (*non accedes ad orationem cum conscientia mala*)

As with 2.7 above, the Greek's admonition to "disclose your wrongdoings (ἐξομολογήσῃ τὰ παραπτώματά)" finds no parallel in Doct and looks suspiciously like community instructions not typical of the Latin tradition. Once more it is likely that H reflects a secondary adaptation unique to the Greek manuscript tradition and not present in the original text.

A comparison of manuscript traditions, regardless of where the Latin stands historically with respect to the Greek, sheds significant insight into the evolution of the primary document H. This is reinforced by the fact that only minor discrepancies occur between the two traditions with respect to detail of wording and phraseology. Most clearly, the hands that touched each tradition are different in perspective and tone; readers of the *Didache* must pay special attention to such concerns.

COPTIC

A single section of text remains in Coptic (Fayumic, probably based on a Sahidic *Vorlage*), having been discovered in Cairo in 1923 and subsequently transferred to London, where it remains today in the British Museum under the designation British Museum, *Oriental* 9271 (Horner 1924, 225–31; Schmidt 1925, 81–99; Lefort 1952, ix–xv). This single papyrus page dates from the fourth or fifth century, and features three columns of text from 10.3b–12.2a printed with two columns on the recto (horizontal papyrus strands) and a half column on the verso (vertical papyrus strands). The text begins at the top of the page, but concludes mid-column on the opposite side in an odd fashion, as though the copyist either chose not to include additional materials after 12.2a or did not have them available. Theories abound that the piece is an excerpt (Schmidt 1925, 81–82 [attributed to Bell]), a translation exercise (Adam 1957, 26), the concluding segment of a longer papyrus roll (Jefford and Patterson 1989–90, 67), or simply a writing exercise (Schmidt 1925, 81–99; Jones and Mirecki 1995, 87; Niederwimmer 1998, 24–25 n. 15).

The materials contained here relate to the eucharistic prayers of chapter 10 (beginning midway through) and instructions on itinerant apostles and prophets who visit the community. The earlier materials are the more interesting, since they include features not paralleled elsewhere. Two examples will suffice to illustrate this difference. The first of these is the intended distinction between "insiders" and "outsiders" from the perspective of Copt:

Did 10.3

H   and gave food and drink to humanity . . . but favored us with spiritual food and drink (τροφήν τε καὶ ποτὸν ἔδωκας τοῖς ἀνθρώποις . . . ἡμῖν δὲ ἐχαρίσω πνευματικὴν τροφὴν καὶ ποτόν)

Copt   and gave them to the children of humanity . . . but <as for us>, you favored us, you gave us spiritual food and drink (ϩακτειτογ ⲛⲉⲛϣⲏⲣⲓ ⲛⲛⲗⲱϩⲓ . . . ⲁⲛⲟⲛ ⲇⲉ ϩⲁⲕⲉⲣϩⲙⲁⲧ ⲛⲉⲛ ϩⲁⲕϯ ⲛⲉⲛ ⲛⲟⲩϩⲣⲏ ⲙⲙⲡⲛⲉⲩⲙⲁⲧⲓⲕⲱⲛ)

A subtle distinction exists between H and Copt here. H indicates that humanity, which previously was provided material nourishment, can now obtain spiritual nourishment through God's child. Copt indicates that, while humanity (lit., "sons of men") is provided material nourishment, "we alone" (="the favored") receive spiritual nourishment. A distinction between two separate groups is thus provided in Copt that is not indicated by the tradition behind H.

The second example relates to the blessing of the ointment that appears in Copt at 10.7 after the instruction to permit prophets to "give thanks" as they wish. No parallel exists elsewhere in the tradition:

Did 10.7

Copt   But concerning the saying for the ointment, give thanks as you say: We thank you, Father, for the ointment that you showed us through Jesus your son . . . (ⲉⲧⲃⲉ ⲡⲥⲉ ϫⲓ ⲛ̄ⲗⲉ ⲛⲙⲡⲉⲥⲧⲓⲛⲟⲩϥⲓ ϣⲉⲡϩⲙⲁⲧ ⲛ̄ⲧⲉⲓϩⲏ ⲉⲧⲉⲧⲛϫⲱ ⲙⲁⲥ ϫⲉ ⲧⲉⲛϣⲉⲡϩⲙⲁⲧ ⲛ̄ⲧⲁⲁⲕ ⲡϣⲧ ⲉⲧⲃⲉ ⲡⲉⲥϯⲛⲟⲩϥⲓ ⲉⲧⲉϩⲁⲕ ⲧⲁⲙⲁⲛ ⲉⲗⲁϥ ⲉⲃⲁⲗ ϩⲓⲧⲛ ⲓⲏⲥ̄ ⲡⲉⲕϣⲏⲣⲓ . . .)

This prayer was previously known from ApCon at the same position in the text, thus suggesting that its location at the conclusion of the eucharistic prayers of the tradition's liturgical sequence is quite old. Most scholars believe that its presence here is not original, however, having entered the tradition sometime after the year 200 (Vööbus 1968, 41–59; Klinghardt 1996, 465–76; cf. Gero 1977, 67–84; Wengst 1984, 82–83). This and similar ointment prayers from antiquity were widely known and indicate popular usage within church liturgies, particularly in the region of Egypt.

Apart from its attestation to a slightly different form of the eucharistic prayers, Copt remains relatively close to H and supports its basic reading of those petitions that have been preserved, as well as instructions on how to receive outsiders into the community. It is clear that the Greek and Coptic reflect the same institutional conventions, though the differences between these two literary strands do not clearly indicate which of the two represents the more original form of the tradition.

ETHIOPIC

A version of either the Greek or Coptic tradition of the *Didache* was eventually translated into Ethiopic, though only portions of that work have been preserved. The remainder includes Did 8.1–2a; 11.3–5, 7–12; 12.1–13.1, 3–7, which has been inserted secondarily into the *Ethiopian Church Order*, canons 49–52 (hereafter: Eth). The likely date for this tradition is sometime in the fourth century (Horner 1924, 401–2; Audet 1958, 43; Giet 1970, 16–17; Niederwimmer 1989, 26 n. 32).

GEORGIAN

The only witness to a Georgian tradition for the *Didache* is attested by a single journal article from the early twentieth century (Peradse 1932, 111–16). The author of that piece, Gregor Peradse, offers the collation of a Georgian manuscript (copied by Simon Pheikrishvili in 1923) against the Greek text of H as rendered in the work of Adolf von Harnack. Peradse noted that the text itself came from the early nineteenth century and was ultimately destroyed, thus leaving no evidence for consideration except the brief record of the collation.

Differences between Geor and H are limited, though some aspects of this modern rendering are worth consideration. Geor lacks 1.5–6 (already considered a possible secondary addition to H together with 1.3b–4 and 2.1) and 13.5–7 (concluding words on visiting prophets). Further, Geor offers "paraphrasing additions" throughout that give a more complete sense to the text, as well as a brief conclusion at 16.8 not otherwise preserved by H or attested by indirect manuscript traditions such as ApCon or CO (Niederwimmer 1998, 27).

The extent to which Geor should be incorporated into considerations of the evolving textual tradition behind the *Didache* is highly disputed. Many scholars note the text but do not accept its limited evidence to be useful for significant corrections to the textual tradition known from other manuscripts (Rordorf and Tuilier 1998, 115 n. 2), while other researchers include its testimony with caution (Giet 1970, 18; Niederwimmer 1998, 26–27). The latter approach is likely the more reasonable, especially since the Georgian (if indeed authentic) offers only minor elements for consideration.

THE *DIDACHE* IN THE *APOSTOLIC CONSTITUTIONS*

The principal indirect witness to the *Didache* is found in Book 7 of the fourth-century *Apostolic Constitutions*. Intended to serve as a code of instruction and of moral and liturgical law, the work incorporates much of the *Didache* into 7.1.2–32.4 as the basis of the author's teachings. The text has been greatly enhanced, however, incorporating scriptural passages as support for certain instructions and adding editorial comments as the justification for various comments.

These adaptations are evident from the very beginning of the section: 7.1 begins with quotations from Deut 30:19, 1 Kgs 18:21, Matt 6:24, and 1 Tim 4:10 before moving to the teaching of the "two ways" known from Did 1.1–6.1. This tendency to incorporate scripture is continued throughout, as is illustrated at 7.2.4, where the reader is told to "turn also the other [cheek]" (Did 1.4) as supported by an appeal to the words of King David from Ps 7:5. Editorial comments are often similar in their scriptural focus, as at 7.2.12, where one reads "do not steal" (Did 2.2), which is buttressed by the author's recollection of the thefts by Achan (Joshua 7) and Gehazi (2 Kings 5).

Apart from the voluminous nature of these additions throughout the writing, the author seems otherwise to have omitted materials known from the text of H. One notes, for example, that Did 1.5b–2.1 is not included here, nor is the wording of 6.2. The former omission is problematic for those who argue that the whole of Did 1.3b–2.1 is secondary to the textual tradition, since ApCon is clearly aware of the materials from 1.3b–5a ("bless those who curse you . . . for the father wants each one to be given . . ."). The omission of 6.2 may simply reflect the author's disagreement with the teaching of the *Didache* (Niederwimmer 1989, 28), but it is equally likely that the materials in H result from an editorial insertion that occurred after its use by ApCon. Finally, the eschatological materials that conclude the *Didache* (16.1–8) are missing from these materials, undoubtedly because they do not fit with the purpose of the work.

ApCon is very important as a guide to understanding H, especially when the latter manuscript diverges from Doct. At the same time, however, it is necessary to recognize that the author of ApCon uses the *Didache* source in a very unconstrained manner, adding other materials when deemed desirable (as seen above) and perhaps paraphrasing on occasion. It is extremely difficult to judge the author's use of the *Didache* on these occasions. A good example occurs with respect to the liturgical traditions of ApCon, which are not always in full agreement with those in H. This is illustrated in 7.22.2, where the author includes a ritual for anointing with "holy oil" (ἔλαιον) followed by "ointment" (μύρον) prior to baptism, neither of which is mentioned in H. The "ointment" is indeed included elsewhere in the instructions of the Coptic text, but in reference to the eucharistic prayers, and may have thus been original to the tradition at some juncture in the text (Niederwimmer 1989, 28).

Several subsequent literary traditions depend on ApCon, including the *Fragmenta Anastasiana* and the *Sentences* of Isaac the Syrian. Though each of these works shows familiarity with the "two ways" tradition known by both H and ApCon, they are primarily dependent on the latter and thus of less benefit in any evaluation of the literary evolution of the *Didache* (Giet 1970, 140–42).

In addition to Book 7 of ApCon, some scholars have viewed the literary source behind Books 1–6—that is, the *Didascalia apostolorum* (Dida), known in both Syriac and Latin—as a likely witness to the text of the *Didache* as well. The nature of the evidence is somewhat tenuous and is highly debated, but if such attributions may be accepted, the early provenance of the *Didascalia* within the third century would make the work one of our oldest known witnesses to the tradition of the *Didache* (Connolly 1923, 147–57; Giet 1970, 143–45). The writing is thus included in the reconstruction of source materials given in the notes below.

THE *DIDACHE* IN *APOSTOLIC CHURCH ORDER* AND *EPITOME OF THE CANONS OF THE HOLY APOSTLES*

The early fourth-century *Apostolic Church Order* (CO; or *Ecclesiastical Canons of the Holy Apostles*) includes a parallel to *Didache* 1–4 in chapters 4–13, itself the opening section of a longer manual of instruction. Like Doct, however, it omits the materials that now appear in Did 1.3b–2.1, reinforcing the belief that those have been added secondarily to the tradition, as well as the concluding "way of death" instructions that are preserved in *Didache* 5.

The *Epitome* (Epit) appears as Book 8 of ApCon and likewise preserves a version of the "two ways" materials similar to that form found in CO (Funk 1905, 460–595). It is difficult to know by comparison if one author has made use of the other or, more likely, if they share a common version of the *Didache* as a source (van de Sandt and Flusser 2002, 64).

Each text focuses on the teachings of the "two ways" (minus the "way of death" materials), omits the text of Did 1.3b–2.1, and places the materials in the mouths of eleven disciples as the presumed source of the teachings. Materials associated with moral teachings are attributed to the apostle John, while those associated with ecclesiastical laws are given over to the apostle Peter. They tend to read similarly in their understanding of the text, oftentimes in agreement against H and ApCon. This holds true throughout, but is especially interesting in comparison with the final teachings of *Didache* 4, where the order of the concluding elements varies between CO and Epit (so, 4.9, 14a, 13a, 14b, 12, 13b, and 14c).

THE *DIDACHE* IN THE ARABIC *LIFE OF SHENOUTE*

A weaker witness to the "two ways" section of the *Didache* appears in the Arabic *Life of Shenoute*. This text, like CO before it, omits both Did 1.3b–2.1 and 4.9–14. It also contains numerous features that are not typical of H and the Greek tradition. For example, the "my child" sayings of Did 3.1–6 begin already in 2.6 and continue through 4.8 (except for 3.9–10 and 4.7). References to "Jesus" at 4.7 and to "Jesus Christ" at 2.5 and 4.14 indicate a Christianization of the text and subsequent editing to the tradition of H (van de Sandt and Flusser 2002, 67).

There is some reason to believe that the Arabic tradition is dependent on an early Coptic *Vorlage*, though the details of this tradition remain uncertain. Scholars generally believe the work to be an embellishment of a Sahidic Coptic archetype, with a revision perhaps from the seventh century (van de Sandt and Flusser 2002, 67). The antiquity of the manuscript tradition behind the text is undoubtedly old, however, as suggested by the primitive nature of the language and the omissions of materials that appear in the later manuscript of H.

A NEW TRANSLATION

The *Didache* has appeared in numerous translations since its original publication by Bryennios in 1883. Older versions still serve as ready resources for casual readers of the text in English (Alexander and Donaldson 1867–73; Lake 1912), yet the form and wording are now antiquated. Newer efforts have made the writing accessible to a wider academic audience, catering to postmodern tastes and sensitivities (Cody 1995; Ehrman 2003; Holmes 2007) and offering insightful comments on the manuscript traditions, whose difficulties make the *Didache* unique within ancient Christian literature.

The present translation offers several benefits over contemporary presentations of the text of the *Didache*. The primary manuscript witness of Codex Hierosolymitanus is given on the left side of the page with alternate readings from the *Doctrina*, POxy 1782, and Coptic tradition as presented on the right. The latter texts generally do not overlap in the materials they preserve, which makes their comparative readings easily envisaged on the page. The single exception is that the latter half of POxy 1782 intersects with the *Doctrina*, in which case the translation favors the presentation of the *Doctrina* with pertinent comments on the POxy fragment listed in the notes. Fortunately, such divergences are few. Original-language terminology is provided in Greek and Coptic font where appropriate, though Ethiopian and Georgian words are indicated through use of their Greek equivalents only.

Gender-neutral language is included wherever possible in order to respect the sensitivities of the contemporary reader. The assumption here is that, even though male-specific language dominates ancient references to both people and God, the Didachist applied the majority of teachings to everyone regardless of sex. This is admittedly not always clear in the biblical narrative, as with the case of God's presentation of the Torah to Moses and the seventy elders at Mt. Sinai, a scene in which the elders represent the *men* of ancient Israel, who themselves serve as representatives of homes and families, for which they are responsible. In this particular instance the covenant is likely intended to be enacted between the deity and males of the twelve tribes on behalf of all people (including women, children, slaves, and even livestock) within the community. No such assumptions are evident within the *Didache*, however, and thus no similar conflict in perception exists for the translation.

In addition, there is a concerted effort to avoid as much contemporary theological bias in the translation as possible, in deference to the assumption that the foundational traditions and sources behind the text are extremely early within the tradition and thus do not necessarily share the ecclesiastical and doctrinal biases of later post-Constantinian theology. For example, the translation preserves the ambiguity of the Greek term παῖς, which may be rendered as "servant, son, child," in favor of "child" both with reference to the figures of David (cf. 9.2) and Jesus (cf. 9.2–3; 10.2–3). No distinction is indicated to signal that the author intends a different connotation for either David or Jesus based on theological presuppositions. The Coptic word ⲡⲉⲕϣⲏⲣⲓ is rendered appropriately as "your son" at the same place, however, as a reflection of the specifically masculine form of that tradition. Admittedly, the phrase "in the name of the Father and of the Son and of the Holy Spirit" (7.1, 3) must be retained as something of an evolutionary peculiarity within the text. The phrase is rare in NT literature (perhaps a later addition?) and unique within other writings of late first- and second-century literature. Its presence in the *Didache* is difficult to explain in this regard if the text is indeed to be attributed to the earliest Christian situation. Likewise, the rare use of the term "Christian" (Χριστιανός) found in 12.4 is not otherwise widely encountered early in the literature with some few exceptions in the NT and scattered early second-century usages. Finally, references to the "gospel" (εὐαγγέλιος) in 8.2, 11.3, and 15.3–4 are among the oldest such allusions in Christian literature and may perhaps indicate a specific written text (in which case they would indeed be the earliest indicators of the literary tradition).

These elements—Trinitarian formula, reference to "Christian," references to "gospel"—indicate that a second hand may be at work within the text representing a later (if not dramatically so) contribution to the *Didache*'s earlier perspective on the ancient Christian community. Such unusual features do not necessarily require any reconsideration of the translation, since the entirety of the text should still be dated quite early by contemporary standards, certainly prior to the influences of evolved late second-century theological concerns, such as those found in the works of Irenaeus or the subsequent heresiologists of the third and fourth centuries.

Peculiar to the *Didache*, the text shifts often between use of the second person singular and plural pronouns. A few recent translators have chosen to signal these transitions with use of an umlaut as an indicator of plural constructions, as in "ÿou" (meaning "all of you") or "präy" (meaning "all of you pray") (Milavec 2003; Varner 2005). This practice is not followed here. Instead, specific notes to the user indicate shifts from the singular to plural, to avoid complicating the translation.

Also, editors generally have a tendency to insert a definite pronoun at those places where such might be expected by the reader according to the standards of contemporary usage and doctrinal confession, as with the phrase "honor that one as *the* Lord" (4.1). The Greek of the *Didache* often omits such terminology, perhaps to suggest that a somewhat different nuance is intended on certain occasions, as with "honor that one as Lord" (ὡς κύριον). When such nuancing is conceivably intended by the author, the present translation does not employ a definite article. At other times when the definite article is clearly expected for an accurate reading, it is included with pointed brackets, as with "for wherever one speaks of <the> Lord, there <the> Lord is" (4.1). Thus the reader may make decisions either for or against the present translation according to personal taste with the assurance that the words given on the page reflect a clear reading of the manuscripts themselves.

In addition to these features, specific original-language words are provided throughout the translation to indicate the terminology in use by the authors of the manuscripts. Sometimes this is offered simply for the convenience of the reader, as with Doct 1.1, where the phrase "in <the> world" is accompanied by the original Latin (*in saeculo*) to indicate the author's use of terminology not paralleled in the primary text of H. At other times two parallel terms are given in order for the reader to compare manuscript readings, as with Did 1.3, where H reads "you love (ἀγαπᾶτε) the ones . . ." and POxy 1782 offers alternatively "you love (φιλεῖτε) the ones . . ." Such variances in meaning might not otherwise be detected from the translation itself.

Furthermore, two aspects of translation are not easily indicated from a reading of the text alone and thus are addressed in the Additional Notes of the volume. The first of these situations arises from the text's use of scripture. While a surface reading seems to reveal numerous passages from both Old and New Testament writings, the context in which those sources appear is without clear definition. In comparison with manuscripts that preserve the *Didache* in a form older than that of H for example (one thinks especially of the fourth-century *Apostolic Constitutions*), such references are occasionally omitted. This situation is particularly troublesome, since the author of ApCon is prone to employ scripture effusively as an explanation for the rationale behind the teachings of the *Didache* and thus might be expected to preserve the same from the source tradition. In such instances the view is offered within the additional notes that the scriptural citations known from H are in fact secondary to the original text of the Didachist, and thus should not be considered as typical of that author's perspective.

Secondly, while the Didachist makes frequent use of terminology known either from scriptural parallels (both the LXX and NT) or from classical literature outside the biblical tradition, several terms and phrases are either unique to the *Didache* or are used uniquely within the text. One might note by way of example the use of a term like "to acknowledge, confess" (προσεξομολογέω; 14.1), which is the only true *hapax legomenon* in the *Didache*. Otherwise there are terms such as "vulgar" (αἰσχρολόγος; 3.3) and "grumbler" (γόγγυσος; 3.3), which are not found in Greek literature prior to the *Didache* but only in subsequent literature. So too, several words in the *Didache* are paralleled in the NT but employed differently by the Didachist, as for example with "give an account" (here translated as "explain why"; δώσει δίκην; 1.5) and "jealous" (ζηλωτής; 3.2). The former term, "account" (δίκη), typically indicates some negative dimension of "judgment" or "punishment" within the NT, but carries a morally neutral sense in the perspective of the Didachist. Traditionally, the latter term is rendered in a positive sense within scripture, often translated by the English equivalent "zeal," but its context within the *Didache* clearly is negative, an attitude to be avoided. The additional notes serve as important aides by which to understand such subtleties in the text, though in certain instances the reader might wish to consult more exhaustive treatments of the text and its manuscript traditions for additional information about specific terms and phrases.

Finally, certain words are often rendered in a more neutral sense than is typically translated either in scripture or other Christian literature. Specifically, the term ψυχή is rendered as "self" rather than "spirit" in order not to heighten any unintended religious undertones within the text. Similarly, the word ἐκκλησία is typically translated as "assembly" rather than "church" so that no inadvertent prejudice associated with contemporary views of that institution may be read back into the assumptions of the Didachist anachronistically. In all such cases these words are marked within the translation in order to alert the reader.

HOW TO USE THIS BOOK

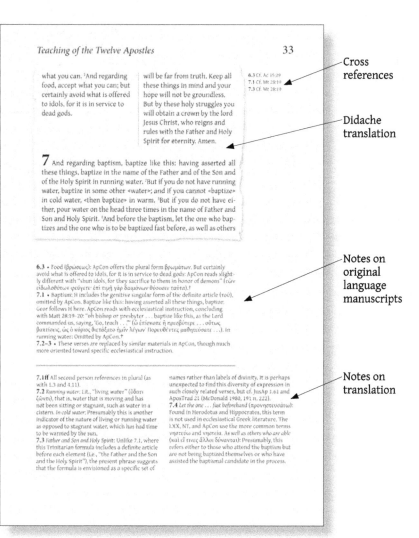

what you can. ³And regarding food, accept what you can; but certainly avoid what is offered to idols, for it is in service to dead gods.

will be far from truth. Keep all these things in mind and your hope will not be groundless. But by these holy struggles you will obtain a crown by the lord Jesus Christ, who reigns and rules with the Father and Holy Spirit for eternity. Amen.

6.3 Cf. Ac 15:29
7.1 Cf. Mt 28:19
7.3 Cf. Mt 28:19

Cross references

Didache translation

7 And regarding baptism, baptize like this: having asserted all these things, baptize in the name of the Father and of the Son and of the Holy Spirit in running water. ²But if you do not have running water, baptize in some other ‹water›; and if you cannot ‹baptize› in cold water, ‹then baptize› in warm. ³But if you do not have either, pour water on the head three times in the name of Father and Son and Holy Spirit. ⁴And before the baptism, let the one who baptizes and the one who is to be baptized fast before, as well as others

6.3 • Food (βρώσεως): ApCon offers the plural form βρωμάτων. But certainly avoid what is offered to idols, for it is in service to dead gods: ApCon reads slightly different with "shun idols, for they sacrifice to them in honor of demons" (τῶν εἰδωλοθύτων φεύγετε· ἐπὶ τιμῇ γὰρ δαιμόνων θύουσιν ταῦτα).†
7.1 • Baptism: H includes the genitive singular form of the definite article (τοῦ), omitted by ApCon. Baptize like this: having asserted all these things, baptize: Geor follows H here. ApCon reads with ecclesiastical instruction, concluding with Matt 28:19-20: "oh bishop or presbyter . . . baptize like this, as the Lord commanded us, saying, 'Go, teach . . .'" (ᾧ ἐπίσκοπε ἢ πρεσβύτερε . . . οὕτως βαπτίσεις, ὡς ὁ κύριος διετάξατο ἡμῖν λέγων Πορευθέντες μαθητεύσατε . . .), in running water: Omitted by ApCon.†
7.2-3 • These verses are replaced by similar materials in ApCon, though much more oriented toward specific ecclesiastical instruction.

Notes on original language manuscripts

7.1ff All second person references in plural (as with 1.3 and 4.11).
7.2 *Running water*: Lit., "living water" (ὕδατι ζῶντι), that is, water that is moving and has not been sitting or stagnant, such as water in a cistern. *In cold water*: Presumably this is another indicator of the nature of living or running water as opposed to stagnant water, which has had time to be warmed by the sun.
7.3 *Father and Son and Holy Spirit*: Unlike 7.1, where this Trinitarian formula includes a definite article before each element (i.e., "the Father and the Son and the Holy Spirit"), the present phrase suggests that the formula is envisioned as a specific set of

names rather than labels of divinity. It is perhaps unexpected to find this diversity of expression in such closely related verses, but cf. JusAp 1.61 and AposTrad 21 (McDonald 1980, 101 n. 222).
7.4 *Let the one . . . fast beforehand* (προνηστευσάτω): Found in Herodotus and Hippocrates, this term is not used in ecclesiastical Greek literature. The LXX, NT, and ApCon use the more common terms νηστεύω and νηστεία. *As well as others who are able* (καὶ εἴ τινες ἄλλοι δύνανται): Presumably, this refers either to those who attend the baptism but are not being baptized themselves or who have assisted the baptismal candidate in the process.

Notes on translation

TEACHING OF THE TWELVE APOSTLES
Teaching of <the> Lord to the Nations
through the Twelve Apostles

[Codex Hierosolymitanus 54]

1 There are two ways—one of life and one of death.

And <there is> a great difference between the two ways. ²So (μὲν οὖν) the way of life is this: first, love God who

[*Doctrina apostolorum*]

1 There are two ways in <the> world (*in saeculo*)—life and death, light and darkness. Two angels are placed over them— one over what is right, another over what is flawed.

And there is a great difference between the two ways. ²The way of life is this: first, love eternal (*aeternum*) God

1.1 Cf. Dt 30:15; Prv 12:28; Jer 21:8; Jb 33:14; Sir 15:17; Mt 7:13–14
1.2 Cf. ªDt 6:5; Sir 7:30; Mt 22:37; Mk 12:30; Lk 10:27a Cf. ᵇLv 19:18; Mt 22:39; Mk 12:31; Lk 10:27b; Gal 5:14; Jas 2:8; Th 25 Cf. ªTob 4:15; Mt 7:12; Lk 6:31

Title • Teaching of the Twelve Apostles (Διδαχὴ τῶν δώδεκα ἀποστόλων): Doct renders this as De Doctrina Apostolorum; Nicephorus, Stichometria offers Διδαχὴ τῶν ἀποστόλων; Athansius, Epistula festales 39 has Διδαχὴ καλουμένη τῶν ἀποστόλων; and EcclHist 3.25 says τῶν ἀποστόλων αἱ λεγόμεναι Διδαχαί. The title may be derived from a reading of Acts 2:42: "And they gave themselves to the teaching and fellowship of the apostles, to breaking bread and prayer" (ἦσαν δὲ προσκαρτεροῦντες τῇ διδαχῇ τῶν ἀποστόλων καὶ τῇ κοινωνίᾳ, τῇ κλάσει τοῦ ἄρτου καὶ ταῖς προσευχαῖς). Some form of the shorter title is likely more original, though certain editors favor the longer (Schaff 1885, 162).
Teaching of the Lord . . . Twelve Apostles (Διδαχὴ κυρίου διὰ τῶν δώδεκα ἀποστόλων τοῖς ἔθνεσιν): This longer title appears in H as the first line of the text.
1.1 • And <there is> a great difference between the two ways: Barn (18.1) omits "between" (μεταξὺ), as does Epit (καὶ διαφορὰ πολλὴ τῶν δύο) and ApCon (πολὺ τὸ διάφορον), which add variations in detail. Doct reads in his constituti sunt angeli duo, unus aequitatis, alter iniquitatis.
1.2 • So the way of life is this: Barn reads "light" for "life" (ἡ οὖν ὁδὸς τοῦ φωτός); while Epit omits "way" (ἡ οὖν τῆς ζωῆς). ApCon offers "thus first happens <to be> the way of life" (πρωτή οὖν τυγχάνει ἡ ὁδὸς τῆς ζωῆς καί).

1.1 *One over what is right, another over what is flawed* (*unus aequitatis alter iniquitatis*): Doct carries a weight of justice and judgment that transcends

that of the Greek text.
1.2 All second person references in singular.

1.3 Cf. Mt 5:44, 46–47; Lk 6:27–28, 32–33, 35

made you; second, your neighbor as yourself. And whatever you might not want to happen to you, similarly (καὶ) do not do to another. ³And the teaching (διδαχή) of these words is this: bless those who curse you and pray for your enemies; and fast for your persecutors. For how is it helpful (ποία γὰρ χάρις) if you love the ones who love you? Do not even the nations do the same (τὸ αὐτὸ)? But you, you love (ἀγαπᾶτε) the ones who hate you and you will have no enemy.

who made you; second, your neighbor as yourself. And whatever you might not want done (*fieri*) to you, do not do to another. ³And the explanation (*interpretatio*) of these words is this:

[POxy 1782]
. . . Do not even the nations do this (τοῦτο)? But you, you love (φιλεῖτε) the ones who hate you and you will have no enemy. Listen to what is neces-

---

First, love God who made you: Doct enhances the name of God with eternal, and ApCon likewise with "<the> lord" (ἀγαπᾶν κύριον τὸν θεόν). Barn and CO add the clause "you shall glorify the one who redeemed you from death" (δοξάσεις τόν σε λυτρωσάμενον ἐκ θανάτου).† Second: CO and Epit replicate the use of "love" (δεύτερον ἀγαπήσεις). ApCon adds "and" (καί) again for completion. Yourself: ApCon, CO, and Epit all read the third person masculine "himself" (ἑαυτόν). And whatever you might not want to happen to you: Slight variations are offered by Epit (πᾶν ὃ μὴ θέλης γενέσθαι σοι) and CO (πάντα ὅσα ἂν μὴ θέλης σοι γίνεσθαι), though the meaning is stable. Similarly do not do to another: Alternative readings occur in ApCon (καὶ σὺ τοῦτο ἄλλῳ οὐ ποιήσεις), as well as in CO and Epit (μηδὲ σὺ ἄλλῳ ποιήσῃς).†
1.3 • And the teaching of these words is this: This phrase is missing in ApCon and Epit, perhaps suggesting its later addition to H. Even the nations do the same (καὶ τὰ ἔθνη τὸ αὐτὸ ποιοῦσιν): POxy reads "this" (τοῦτο), reflecting optional manuscript traditions of Matt 5:46, while ApCon offers a further variation in wording with "for even the nations do this" (καὶ γὰρ οἱ ἐθνικοὶ τοῦτο ποιοῦσιν); cf. JusAp 1.15 (with πόρνοι for ἐθνικοί). If you love the ones who love you (ἐὰν ἀγαπᾶτε τοὺς ἀγαπῶντας ὑμᾶς): ApCon offers the alternative term for "love" with ἐὰν φιλῆτε τοὺς φιλοῦντας ὑμᾶς. Do the same (τὸ αὐτὸ): POxy reads "do this" (τοῦτο). Love (ἀγαπᾶτε) the ones who hate you: POxy and ApCon offer the variant term for "love" (φιλεῖτε). And you will have no enemy (οὐχ ἕξετε ἐχθρόν): Dida reads with H (et inimicum nullum habetis), while ApCon has a different word order (ἐχθρόν οὐχ ἕξετε), likely based on Luke 4:27–28 and Matt 5:44–45. Both H and Dida employ this remark as a comment on the negative form of the "golden rule" cited in 1.2 (Connolly 1923, 148).†

1.3 All second person references in plural.

[4]Reject (ἀπέχου) the appeals (ἐπιθυμιῶν) of the flesh and body. If someone strikes you on the right cheek, turn also the other—and you shall be satisfied. If someone pressures you to go one mile, go two. If someone takes your robe, give also your tunic. If someone takes from you what is yours (τὸ σόν), do not be anxious—for you must not! [5]Give to each one who asks of you and do not be anxious. For the Father wants each one to be given from his own gifts (χαρισμάτων). Fortunate is the one who gives according to <this> instruction (ἐντολή), for that one is without guilt. Woe to the one who receives! For sary for you to do to save your spirit: first of all, disengage (ἀπόσχου) from the appeals of the flesh.

1.4 Cf. [a]1Pt 2:11
Cf. [b]Mt 5:39–42, 48; Lk 6:29–30
1.5 Cf. [a]Mt 5:42; Lk 6:30
Cf. [b]Ac 20:35
Cf. [c]2Th 3:10
Cf. [d]Mt 5:26; Lk 12:59

1.4 • Reject (ἀπέχου): H and ApCon agree on this form. POxy reads "disengage." Of the flesh and body (τῶν σαρκικῶν καὶ σωματικῶν): H and Geor agree on this reading. ApCon reads "of the flesh and world" (καὶ κοσμικῶν), while POxy says only "of the flesh" (τῶν σαρκικῶν). The context argues against any sexual overtones behind this comment (Knopf 1920, 8; Schöllgen 1991, 101).† For you must not (οὐδὲ γὰρ δύνασαι): ApCon omits this phrase, while Geor reads with the addition "for you are not able to do this, even for the sake of faith" (οὐδὲ γὰρ δύνασαι τοῦτο ποιεῖν καὶ τῆς πίστεως ἕνεκα). Cf. 1 Cor 6:1; Giet 1970, 59.
1.5–6 • Give to each . . . whom you give": Geor omits these verses.
1.5 • Woe to the one who receives! (οὐαὶ τῷ λαμβάνοντι): Based on its use of Dida (vae autem his qui habent et cum dolo accipiunt, aut qui possunt sibi iuvare

---

1.4ff All second person references in singular (as with 1.2).
1.4 *Reject the appeals of the flesh and body*: This is not seen in the classical sense of conflict between passion and reason; see e.g., 4 Maccabees. Instead, the materials that follow define the sense here—the listener must not respond to hostility as common expectations might demand, but should harbor higher aspirations. Cf. 1 John 2:15; Titus 2:12; 2 Clem 17.3. *And you shall be satisfied* (καὶ ἔσῃ τέλειος): Typically translated "complete" or "perfect" (cf. 16.2), the context begs for the concept of "fulfilled," perhaps in a Stoic sense. *One mile:*

Originally a Roman mile or thousand steps, ultimately eight stades (or 4,854 feet). *Do not be anxious* (μὴ ἀπαίτει): Typically translated as "do not demand it," the issue is one of desire over ownership rather than ability to reclaim the property in question. *For you must not* (οὐδὲ γὰρ δύνασαι): This is a verisimilitude rather than a moral command (i.e., "don't") with respect to one's inability (i.e., "you are unable"). It is again a rejection of the natural inclinations of the body.
1.5 *Fortunate is the one who gives* (μακάριος ὁ διδούς): Lit., "blessed is the one who gives" (as found in most translations).†

1.6 Cf. Sir 12:1
2.2 Cf. ªEx 20:13–15;
Dt 5:17–19; Mt 19:18;
Mk 10:19; Lk 18:20
Cf. ᵇDt 18:10
Cf. ᶜEx 20:17; Dt 5:21
2.3 Cf. ªZech 5:3;
Mt 5:33
Cf. ᵇEx 20:16; Dt 5:20;
Mt 19:18; Mk 10:19;
Lk 18:20
Cf. ᶜEx 21:17
(LXX=21:16); Mt 15:4
Cf. ᵈPrv 12:28 LXX;
Zech 7:10; 8:17

certainly, if someone receives who has a need, that one is without guilt; but the one who receives without need will have to explain why and for what cause. And being in prison, that one will be probed about what was done and will not be set free from there until the last penny (κοδράντην) has been paid. ⁶But it has also been said about this: "Let your gift sweat (ἱδρωσάτω) in your hands until (μέχρις) you know to whom you give."

2 And a second instruction (ἐντολή) of the teaching <is this>: ²Do not murder, do not commit adultery, do not corrupt a child, do not be sexually immoral, do not steal, do not practice magic, do not use potions, do not abort a child nor kill a newborn, do not lust for a

[*Doctrina apostolorum* cont.]
²Do not commit adultery, do not murder, do not give false witness, do not corrupt a child, do not practice magic, do not use evil potions, do not abort a child nor kill a newborn, do not crave (*concupisces*) your neighbor's possessions. ³Do not

et accipiunt. Unusquisque vero de accipientibus dabit rationem domino Deo in die iudicii, quare acceperit), ApCon expands this saying considerably elsewhere (4.3) with "woe to those who have, who receive hypocritically or can support themselves, and want to receive from others, for both of them will give account to the Lord God on the day of judgment." Apart from this parallel, Dida is likely dependent here on the parallel in HermMan 2.5–6 (Connolly 1923, 148–49).
1.6 • Let . . . sweat (ἱδρωσάτω): Emended by Bryennios as a scribal error. H reads with the alternative form ἱδρωτάτω meaning "to settle or fix" (ἱδρύω; cf. ἱδρώς in Luke 22:44).† Until (μέχρις): Again emended by Bryennios. H reads μέχρι.
2.2 • Do not be sexually immoral: Omitted by Geor. Do not abort a child nor kill a newborn: Omitted by Epit. H reads "newborn" (γεννηθέντα), though most editors prefer the alternative form γεννηθέν, as emended by Bryennios and supported by CO, ApCon, and Barn (19.5). Cf. Diognetus 5.6; Tacitus, Historiae 5.5–6. A neighbor's possessions: ApCon, Barn, Doct, and Epit add "your" (σοῦ), undoubtedly in sympathy with the phrase "your neighbor as yourself" (1.2).

1.6 *But* (ἀλλὰ . . . δὲ): Bryennios emends H here to read "but . . . indeed" (ἀλλὰ . . . δή), which is

certainly possible but not adopted for the translation here.

neighbor's possessions. ³Do not commit perjury, do not give false testimony, do not speak evil, do not recall evil doings. ⁴Do not be of two minds or double-tongued, because (γὰρ) a double-tongue is a lethal snare. ⁵Your word must be neither false nor empty—but you must act accordingly (μεμεστωμένος πράξει). ⁶You must not be a coveter nor greedy nor a hypocrite nor hateful nor arrogant. You must not conceive an evil plan against your neighbor. ⁷Do not hate anyone—but reprimand some, pray for some—and some you shall love more than yourself (ψυχήν).

commit perjury, do not speak evil, do not recall evil doings. ⁴Do not be duplicitous in giving counsel, nor double-tongued—the tongue is a lethal snare. ⁵Your word must be neither empty nor false. ⁶You must not be lustful (cupidus) nor greedy nor rapacious nor idolatrous nor argumentative nor irritable. Do not entertain evil counsel against your neighbor. ⁷Do not hate anyone; some you shall love more than your soul (animam).

2.4 Cf. ᵃSir 5:14; 6:1; 28:13
Cf. ᵇPrv 21:6
2.7 Cf. Lv 19:17–18; Mt 18:15–17; Jd 22–23

2.3 • Do not speak evil: Omitted by Geor. Do not recall evil doings: ApCon adds here "for a person's own lips are a snare" (Prov 6:2) as a rationale for the warning.

2.4 • Do not be of two minds or double-tongued (οὐκ ἔσῃ διγνώμων οὐδὲ δίγλωσσος): ApCon offers οὐκ ἔσῃ διγνώμος οὐδὲ δίγλωσσος. Dida poses this as a qualification for the office of bishops (2.6.1).

2.5 • False nor empty, but you must act accordingly: ApCon reads here only "false" (ψευδής); Arab has only "false nor empty" (ψευδής οὐ κενός). CO agrees with Doct's reversal of terms (vacuum nec mendax). But you must act accordingly: The omission of this phrase from Doct, ApCon, and CO suggests its secondary insertion into H, perhaps inserted together with "and you shall be satisfied" and "for you must not" in 1.4.†

2.7 • But reprimand some: Though missing in Doct, ApCon offers the more specific phrase "reprimand your brother" (ἐλέγξεις τὸν ἀδελφόν σου) in keeping with "your (σοῦ) neighbor's possessions" in 2.2.† Pray for some: Missing in Doct. POxy and Epit support the reading of H (περὶ δὲ ὧν προσεύσεις), while CO reads "but to some be merciful" (οὓς δὲ ἐλεήσεις).

2.4 *Double-tongued:* The term διγλωσσία used here is not commonly found, though a parallel appears in Prov 1:13 and Barn 19.7 (the witness of Codex Sinaiticus reads γλωσσώδης). Cf. also the related term δίλογοι in Polycarp, *To the Philippians* 5.2. Thucydides used it to mean "to speak in two languages," which led to its use for an "interpreter"

(Plutarch). The emphasis of the author clearly rests on the duplicitous nature of those who speak one way but act another. This concept is equivalent to the warning on the dangers of the tongue in Jas 3:5–10.

2.7 *Yourself:* Lit., "your soul/life" (ψυχήν).

3.1 Cf. 1Th 5:22
3.2–6 Cf. Ex 20:13–
17; Dt 5:17–21; Mt
5:21–37

3 My child, run from each kind of evil and from anything like it. ²Do not be inclined to anger, for anger leads to murder; neither be jealous nor quarrelsome nor hot-tempered, for all these generate murders. ³My child, do not be lustful (ἐπιθυμητής), for lust leads to depravity (πορνείαν); neither be vulgar nor one who lifts up their eyes, for all these

3 Son, run from an evil person and from anyone like that. ²⁻³Do not be inclined to anger, for anger leads to murder; neither be eager for malice nor proud, for each of these breeds anger.

3.1 • My child: Omitted by ApCon and Epit, the phrase has the support of POxy, CO, and the variant "son" (fili) in Doct. Geor adds to this "I say to you for the sake of the Lord" (λέγω σοι ὑπὲρ τοῦ κυρίου), a likely addition based on the recognition that the prohibitions reflect scripture.† Each kind of evil: For the translation "evil," ApCon and Epit agree on the variant reading κακοῦ in place of what was likely the original term πονηροῦ, as supported by H, POxy, and CO. POxy also adds "each kind of evil affair" (πράγματος) for the sake of completion. From anything like it: POxy omits the phrase "from anything" (ἀπὸ παντὸς), though it is otherwise supported by all other parallel texts.
3.2 • For anger leads to murder: Omitted by ApCon. The simple "for" (γάρ) in H and CO appears as "since [anger] leads" in POxy (ἐπειδὴ ὁδηγεῖ) and Doct (quia iracundia ducit). POxy and Doct likely reflect an adaptation from a divergent textual history in opposition to that of H. Epit adds "these things" (ὁδηγεῖ γὰρ ταῦτα) to the phrase, perhaps under the influence of the closing words of the verse: "for all these generate murders" (Wengst 1984, 68). Neither be (μηδέ): H and ApCon agree here against the orthographic variant μήτε in Epit. A further minor alternative appears in the reading "do not be" (μὴ γίνου) of CO. Quarrelsome (ἐριστικός): ApCon here reads "inclined to madness" (μανικός). Hot-tempered (θυμικός): The manuscript traditions show a wide diversity of terminology here, though no significant variation in meaning: CO reads θυμώδης (a variant of θυμοειδής); ApCon offers θρασύς; Epit has μανικός. For all these generate murders: CO reads the slight variant "generate murder" (φόνος γεννᾶται), while ApCon omits the phrase entirely.
3.3 • My child: Omitted by ApCon and Epit. The phrase has the support of POxy and CO, but not Doct (cf. 3.2) since the entire verse is missing. Do not be lust-

3.2 *For all of these generate murders*: The Greek indicates that each of these elements is parallel to anger, thus leading to murder, while Doct ("for each of these breeds anger") envisions that malice and pride lead to anger and, only thereafter presumably, to murder.
3.3 *Vulgar* (αἰσχρολόγος): This term appears for the first time in literature here, though parallels appear in the late second-century writings of Pollux (6.123; 8.80–81) and thereafter in ApCon (7.6) and CO (9). Cf. αἰσχρολογία and αἰσχρότης in the

NT. *One who lifts up their eyes* (ὑψηλόφθαλμος): This is often translated as something like "do not let your eyes roam" or "do not stare brazenly," which is a contemporary parallel in concept. Translated literally, however, the warning is clear, since the action of lowering the chin but lifting the eyes typically indicates lustful or complicit intentions. The only parallel in literature is in CO (9). ApCon (7.6) reads with "leering eyes" (ριψόφθαλμος), which harmonizes well with "adulteries" (μοιχεῖαι) that follows (Schaff 1885, 109).

engender adulteries. ⁴My child, do not be a fortuneteller, since it leads to idolatry; neither be an enchanter nor astrologer nor magician, nor wish to see them, for all these generate idolatry. ⁵My child, do not be a liar, since lying leads to theft; neither be a lover of wealth nor vain, for all these generate thefts. ⁶My child, do not be a grumbler, as it leads to slanderous talk; neither be arrogant or

⁴Do not be an astrologer or enchanter (*delustrator*), which leads to superstition, nor wish to see or hear them. ⁵Do not be a liar, which leads to theft; neither be a lover of wealth nor vain, for each of these leads to thefts. ⁶Do not be a grumbler, which leads to slanderous talk. Do not be ar-

3.4 Cf. Lv 19:26, 31; Dt 18:10–11
3.6 Cf. Wis 1:11; Ph 2:14

ful: ApCon adds "of evil things" (κακῶν). Neither: CO and Epit read instead μὴ γίνου, with CO inserting "child" (τέκνον) first. For all these engender adulteries: Slight variants in wording, though not in meaning, appear with μοιχεῖαι γίνονται in Epit, while the phrase μοιχεῖαι γεννᾶται in CO agrees with the same reading in 3.2. For lust leads to depravity; neither be vulgar nor one who lifts up their eyes, for all of these generate adulteries: This phrase reads differently in ApCon, though the basic sense remains the same: "for lust leads to unending sinning; do not be vulgar nor have a wandering eye nor be drunken, for all of these evils generate adultery."†
3.4 • My child: Omitted by ApCon; Geor omits "my" (μου) only. Since (ἐπειδή): ApCon reads ὅτι. To (εἰς τήν) idolatry: ApCon reads πρός. Neither be an enchanter nor astrologer nor magician: CO and Epit (with slight variation) follow H here. ApCon diverges somewhat with "do not be a charm user or defile your son . . . nor learn evil practices." Nor wish to see them: CO and Geor read with Doct here by including the phrase "or hear them."† For all these generate idolatry: CO reads "idolatries"; Epit has a slight verbal variant.
3.5 • My child: CO omits "my" (μου); Epit omits the entire phrase. Generate thefts: ApCon reads "generate boastful statuses" (ἀλαζονείαι γεννῶνται).
3.6 • My child: CO and Epit omit "my" (μου); ApCon and Epit omit the entire phrase. As it leads to (ὁδηγεῖ εἰς) slanderous talk: CO offers the slight variant ἄγει πρός; ApCon and Epit omit the entire phrase. For all these generate slanderous talk: Epit has a slight verbal variant, while ApCon reads "for all these lead to blasphemy."

3.4 *Fortuneteller* (οἰωνοσκόπος): Lit., "omen watcher." The term is known from Euripides and does not appear in the LXX (except at Isa 47:13 in Theodotion and Symmachus). *Enchanter* (ἐπαοιδός): Used commonly among classical authors (Plato, Euripides, etc.) and the LXX, though NT writers prefer "magician" (μάγος; so Matt 2:1ff) or "magic" (μαγεία; so Acts 8:9, 11; 13:6, 8). *Astrologer* (μαθηματικίς): The word was used early in the sense of "mathematician" (Aristotle), but eventually gained the meaning "astronomical" (Plutarch). Its feminine form μαθηματική was rendered as "astrology" (Socrates), and so by the third century CE the term came to mean "astrologer" (Sextus Empiricus, Porphyry). This meaning ultimately dominated the language of later church councils (Schaff 1885, 102).
3.6 *Grumbler* (γόγγυσος): This word first appears in the *Didache*, though later in ApCon (7.7), CO (11), Theodoret, and Arcadius. Cf. γογγυσμός in Jude 16 for NT usage. *Slanderous talk*: Lit., "blasphemy" (βλασφημία). It is unclear that the author speaks of abusive language against divinity here, however, but instead endorses ethical discourse.

3.7 Cf. Ps 37:11
(LXX=36:11); Mt 5:5
3.8 Cf. Is 66:2
3.10 Cf. Sir 2:4

evil minded, for all these generate slanderous talk. [7]But be
modest (πραΰς), for the modest shall inherit the earth. [8]Be
patient and merciful and in-
nocent and quiet and good, and
at all times respect the words
you have heard. [9]Do not praise
yourself or let yourself (ψυχήν)
be arrogant. Do not attach
yourself to arrogant <people>,
but associate with the righteous and humble. [10]Receive
the things that happen to you
as good, knowing that nothing
happens apart from God.

rogant or evil minded, for each
of these leads to slanderous
talk. [7]Rather, be gentle (*man-
suetus*) insofar as gentle ones
shall possess holy land. [8]Be
patient and fair in commerce,
and respect the words you have
heard. [9]Neither exalt yourself
nor honor yourself among people nor consent, lest your soul
be arrogant, nor attach your
soul to arrogant <people>, but
associate with the righteous
and humble. [10]Whatever happens to you, receive as good,
knowing that nothing happens
apart from God.

3.7 • For the (ἐπεὶ οἱ) modest: CO omits "the" (οἱ); Epit reads "since modest
ones" (ἐπειδή πραεῖς).† The earth: Doct reads sanctam terram; CO has "kingdom of the heavens" (βασιλείαν τῶν οὐρανῶν); Epit offers "kingdom of God"
(βασιλείαν τοῦ θεοῦ).†
3.8 • Be patient and (καί): Both CO and Epit omit "and." Merciful and (καί): Epit
reads "a peacemaker, clean of heart" (εἰρηνοποιός καθαρὸς τὴν καρδίᾳ), to which
CO adds "the heart from each evil thing" (τῇ καρδίᾳ ἀπὸ παντὸς κακοῦ). Quiet
and (ἡσύχιος καί): CO supports H for ἡσύχιος here. ApCon and Epit read with the
more widely used ἡσύχος. CO, ApCon, and Epit all omit "and." Good and (καί):
ApCon omits "and," while CO and Epit add "prudent and" (φυλάσσων καί). And
at all times (διὰ παντός): The omission of this phrase by Doct, ApCon, CO, and
Barn may suggest its secondary insertion into H (Wengst 1984, 70). You have
heard: ApCon reads "of God" (τοῦ θεοῦ), while Geor adds "now" (νῦν).
3.9 • Or let yourself be arrogant: ApCon adds "do not associate <with such>" (οὐ
συμπορεύσῃ). CO reads "or let yourself <be praised>" (τὴν ψυχήν σου). Arrogant
<people> (ὑψηλός): ApCon reads "foolish" (ἀφρόνων). Righteous and humble
(δικαίων καὶ ταπεινῶν): ApCon reads "wise and righteous" (σοφῶν καὶ δικαίων).
3.10 • Receive: CO reads "but (δέ) receive." Receive the things that happen
to you as good (τὰ συμβαίνοντά σοι ἐνεργήματα ὡς ἀγαθὰ προσδέξῃ): ApCon
reads more elegantly, "receive misfortunes that happen to you graciously" (τὰ
συμβαίνοντά σοι πάθη εὐμενῶς δέχου).† Nothing happens apart from God (ἄτερ
θεοῦ οὐδὲν γίνεται): ApCon offers "reward will be given to you by God" (μισθός
σοι παρὰ θεοῦ δοθήσεται . . .), which indicates a more specific "action driven"
rationale for an appropriate lifestyle.

3.8 *And at all times respect the words you have heard*:
This is another verisimilitude as in 1.4 above, all
of which may have been inserted secondarily into
the text. Its presence here breaks the flow of the
discourse.

3.9 *Yourself*: Lit., "your soul/life" (ψυχή; cf. 2.7).
Arrogant (θράσος): Typically translated as "over
boldness," having both positive and negative
meanings in classical usage. The former is preva-
lent in the LXX (cf. "courage" in Acts 28:15).

4 My child, remember night and day the one who speaks God's word to you, and honor that one (αὐτὸν) as Lord. For wherever one speaks of <the> Lord, there <the> Lord is. ²And search out the presence of the holy ones each day, so that you may find comfort in their words. ³Do not [create] disunion, but bring peace to

4 Remember day and night the one who speaks the Lord God's word to you. You shall honor that one (*eum*) as Lord. For wherever <the> Lord is summoned, there <the> Lord is. ²And seek the presence of holy ones, and you will be restored by their words. ³Do not create disunion; bring peace to those in dispute; judge fairly, know-

4.1 Cf. ªSir 7:29–31; Hb 13:7
Cf. ᵇMt 10:40; 18:20
4.2 Cf. ªSir 6:28; 51:26–27; Mt 11:28–29
Cf. ᵇSir 6:34–36
4.3 Cf. Lv 19:15; Dt 1:16–17; Sir 4:9

4.1 • My child: CO omits my (μου); Doct, ApCon, and Epit omit the entire phrase. The one who speaks (τοῦ λαλοῦντός . . .): Co and Epit read "exalt the one who speaks" (τὸν λαλοῦντά . . . ἀγαπήσεις), while ApCon reads "love the one who speaks" (τὸν λαλοῦντά . . . δοξάσεις). Each variation indicates some dissatisfaction with the ambiguity of the verb "to remember" (μιμνήσκω) that follows in H. Remember (μνησθήσῃ): ApCon, CO, and Epit read "and remember him" (δὲ μνησθήσῃ αὐτοῦ), though Epit does not include the conjunction. Night and day (νυκτὸς καὶ ἡμέρας): Doct and ApCon reverse the elements ("day and night"), while CO offers a slight variation in form (νύκτα καὶ ἡμέραν). And honor that one (αὐτὸν): Both Doct and CO omit "and" (δέ). As Lord: H, Doct, and Epit agree on this phrase against CO, which includes the accusative form of "the" (τόν) and is accepted by some scholars (Wengst 1984, 72). ApCon offers a different phrase here, "not as from the same origin, but as the one who is truly your source of support" (οὐχ ὡς γενέσεως αἴτιον, ἀλλ᾽ ὡς τοῦ εὖ εἶναί σοι πρόξενον γενόμενον), which is clearly a nuanced comment by the author reflecting later theological concerns related to Trinitarian speculation. For wherever (ὅθεν γὰρ): ApCon offers a slight variation with ὅπου γάρ. One speaks of <the> Lord: Epit reads "one speaks of Jesus Christ" (Ἰησοῦς Χριστὸς λαλεῖται); ApCon offers "the teachings of God are" (ἡ περὶ θεοῦ διδασκαλία); Doct states "the Lord is brought forth" (unde enim dominica procedunt).† <The> Lord is: ApCon reads "God is present" (ὁ θεὸς πάρεστιν). Geor augments this with "Christ" (Χριστός), clearly added for confessional purposes.†
4.2 • And: Omitted by ApCon. The presence of the holy ones each day: ApCon offers the plural "the faces" (τὰ πρόσωπα) for the singular of H, while CO reads "his presence each day and the other holy ones" (αὐτοῦ καθ᾽ ἡμέραν καὶ τοὺς λοιποὺς ἁγίους). Epit has "him and the other holy ones" (αὐτὸν καὶ τοὺς λοιποὺς ἁγίους).†
4.3 • Do not [create] disunion: Most translators agree with this reading (ποιήσεις σχίσματα) as supported by Doct, ApCon, and CO, or with the variant form ποιήσεις σχίσμα of Epit and Barn, versus "do not desire disunion" (ποθήσεις σχίσμα) in H. But: Omitted by Doct and ApCon. Do not favor <any>: "Any" is likely assumed by H and ApCon, though inserted specifically as τινά by CO, Epit, and Barn. Offenses: Lit., "transgressions." H reads with the plural here, while ApCon, CO, Epit, and Barn all prefer the singular.

4.2 *Presence of the holy ones:* Lit., "the faces of the saints" (τὰ πρόσωπα τῶν ἁγίων). Doct reads similarly (*facies sanctorum*).

4.5 Cf. Sir 4:31; Dt
15:7–8; Ac 20:35
4.6 Cf. Tob 4:8–10
4.7 Cf. Prv 19:17

disputes. Judge fairly; do not favor <any> when considering offenses. ⁴Do not hesitate over the answer. ⁵Do not be like those who extend <their> hands to receive but pull back <so as not> to give. ⁶If you have profited because of your hands, make some reparation (λύτρωσιν) for your sins. ⁷Do not hesitate to give nor gripe while giving, for you can recognize (γνώσῃ) who is a good

ing that you shall be judged. Do not discourage anyone who encounters misfortune. ⁴Do not doubt whether it is true. ⁵Do not be one to extend a hand to receive and pull back <so as not> to return. ⁶If you have gained a ransom (*redemptionem*) for <your> sins, ⁷do not hesitate to give <it> nor mutter, knowing who is a good paymaster of

4.4 • Do not hesitate (οὐ διψυχήεις): Barn offers a slight variant form in οὐ μὴ διψυχήσῃς, while ApCon adds "do not hesitate in your prayer" (οὐ γίνου δίψυχος ἐν προσευχῇ σου), as does CO, "in your prayer do not hesitate" (ἐν προσευχῇ σου μὴ διψυχήσῃς). The texts of ApCon and CO thus suggest a spiritual component not otherwise reflected in H or Barn. Over the answer (πότερον ἔσται ἢ οὔ): ApCon reads "if" (εἰ) for "whether" while Epit offers a more extended comment as further reflected in 4.6, "if you have profited with your hands" (εἰ ἔσται ἔχειν σε ἀπὸ τῶν χειρῶν σου).
4.5 • <Their> hands (τὰς χεῖρας): H, CO, and Barn have the plural form here, while Doct and ApCon offer the singular "hand" (τὴν χεῖρα). Pull back (συσπάω): ApCon reads "draw back" (συστέλλω).
4.6 • Make some reparation (δώσεις λύτρωσιν): CO adds the genitive plural form of "the" (τῶν) to accompany the following "your sins" (ἁμαρτιῶν σου). ApCon reads "give in order that you achieve reparation" (δός, ἵνα ἐργάσῃ εἰς λύτρωσιν); Epit offers the variation "give in order to allow reparation" (δὸς εἰς λύτρωσιν).†
4.7 • Do not hesitate to give: ApCon adds "to a poor one" (πτωχῷ), thus to distinguish those who may justifiably receive charity (cf. 1.6). The good paymaster: Bryennios emends the feminine article ἡ found in H with the masculine form ὁ. This is accepted in the translation here. ApCon omits "good" (καλός).

4.3 *Do not favor <any> when considering offenses:* Lit., "do not choose a person to convict over transgressions" (οὐ λήψῃ πρόσωπον ἐλέγξαι ἐπὶ παραπτώμασιν). *Knowing that you shall be judged* (*sciens quod tu iudicaberis*): Doct returns to the theme of divine oversight as seen already in 3.10.
4.4 *Hesitate* (διψυχέω): This term first appears in the *Didache*, though it is common in subsequent literature. Cf. Barn 19.5; 1 Clem 23.2; HermVis 2.2; ApCon (7.11); CO (13); and Cyril of Alexandria, *In divi Joannis Evangelium* 6. The primary meaning of the term is "to doubt," thus leading to the present translation of not hesitating to provide an answer or, less woodenly, having no uncertainty in one's judgment. *Over the answer:* Lit., "whether it is or

not" (πότερον ἔσται ἢ οὔ). Doct reads *nec dubitabis uerum erit an non erit*, suggesting a situation in which one decides whether someone's misfortune is valid.
4.5 *Pull back:* The verb used here by H means "to draw or squeeze together" (συσπάω), which may mean simply "to close" one's hand, but more likely intends "to draw back or withdraw," as indicated in ApCon.
4.6–7 This is not a separate command on personal redemption, but a comment on 4.5 and 4.8 to the extent that those who themselves have received (even if by their own efforts) must likewise give to others. The instruction in 4.7a almost seems to contradict that of 1.6.

paymaster of wages. ⁸Do not turn away the one in need, but share all things with your brother <or sister> and do not claim anything for yourself; for if you (ἐστε) are sharers in what is permanent (ἀθανάτῳ), how much more in transitory things (θνητοῖς)? ⁹Do not withhold your hand from your son or from your daughter, but teach the fear of God from <their> youth. ¹⁰Do not give orders to your male or female slave—to those who hope in the same God <as you>—when you are angry, so that they do not lose

such wages. ⁸Do not turn away from a needy one, but share all things with your brother <or sister> and do not claim anything for yourself; for if we are (sumus) sharers in <the im>mortal, how much more ought we to be driven by this? For the Lord wants for all to be given from his gifts. ⁹Do not withhold your hand from your sons, but from <their> youth teach them fear of the Lord. ¹⁰Do not give orders when you are angry with your male and female slave, who trust in the same Lord <as you>. Let them

4.8 Cf. ªSir 4:5a
Cf. ᵇAc 2:44–45; 4:32
4.10 Cf. ªSir 4:30a
Cf. ᵇEph 6:9; Col 4:1
Cf. ᶜLk 1:17

4.8 • The one in need (τὸν ἐνδεόμενον): ApCon, CO, Epit, and Doct omit the definite article to read "a needy one" (ἐνδεόμενον). But share all things (συγκοινωνήσεις δὲ πάντα): ApCon reads with the slight variant form κοινωνήσεις εἰς πάντα; CO offers another, κοινωνήσεις ἐν πᾶσιν. For if you are sharers in what is permanent, how much more then in transitory things: ApCon reads "for what all people commonly receive is furnished by God" (κοινὴ γὰρ ἡ μετάληψις παρὰ θεοῦ πᾶσιν ἀνθρώποις παρεσκευάσθη). In what is permanent (ἐν ἀθανάτῳ): CO adds the definite article to read "in the immortal" (ἐν τῳ ἀθανάτῳ), while Geor reads "the spirit of immortality" (ἐν τῇ ἀθανασίᾳ τῇ πνευματικῇ). The term ἀθανάτος appears in classical literature (Homer, Hesiod, etc.) and the LXX, though not in the NT. Cf. Lucian of Samosata, Peregrinus 13.†
4.9 • Teach (διδάξεις): The completion of thought demanded by logic, "teach them" (διδάξεις αὐτούς), is offered by ApCon, Epit, and Doct (docebis eos). The fear of God: While H and ApCon agree on this reading, "of the Lord" (τοῦ κυρίου) is preferred by Epit, Barn, Geor, and Doct (domini). From <their> youth: H, Epit, Barn, and Doct all omit "their" (αὐτῶν), though it is demanded by logic and thus inserted by ApCon.†
4.10 • To those who hope (τοῖς . . . ἐλπίζουσιν): ApCon reads "to those who have trusted" (τοῖς . . . πεποιθόσιν). When you are angry (ἐν πικρίᾳ σου): Lit., "in your anger." Barn omits the term "your" (σου). ApCon offers "in bitterness of soul" (ἐν πικρίᾳ ψυχῆς). So that they do not lose respect for God <who is over you>

4.8 *Do not claim anything for yourself:* Lit., "do not assert things to be separate" (οὐκ ἐρεῖς ἴδια εἶναι). So too Doct (nec dices tua esse). *In what is permanent* (ἐν ἀθανάτῳ): Lit., "in an immortal thing." Doct reads "mortal" (mortalibus), which is likely a non-sensical misreading of the original.
4.10 *When you are angry* (ἐν πικρίᾳ σου): Lit., "in your anger." The phrase "in bitterness of soul"

used by ApCon recalls a phrase known elsewhere in Sir 4.6 ("for if some curse you *in bitterness of soul*, their Maker will hear their prayer"). Use of Sirach here is intriguing, since the Didachist is otherwise keen to employ the work. Explicit citation of Sirach by ApCon in this instance may be a proper rendering of the authentic intention of the Didachist (Wengst 1984, 74).

4.11 Cf. Eph 6:5–8;
Col 3:22–25
4.13 Cf. Dt 4:2; 12:32
(LXX=13:1); Prv 30:6

respect (οὐ μὴ φοβηθήσονται)
for God <who is over you> both.
For <God> does not come to
summon according to status,
but those whom the spirit has
made ready. ¹¹And you slaves,
be obedient to [your] masters
in deference and respect as
exemplary of God (ὡς τύπῳ
θεοῦ). ¹²Hate all hypocrisy and
anything that does not please
the Lord. ¹³Do not abandon the
Lord's instructions, but watch
over what you have received,
neither adding nor subtracting.

fear <both the> Lord and you,
for <the Lord> did not come to
summon according to status,
but <those> in whom he ob-
served the spirit. ¹¹You slaves,
be obedient to your masters
with deference and respect
as exemplary of God (*formae
dei*). ¹²Hate all hypocrisy and
do not do whatever does not
please God. ¹³Therefore, my
son, watch over what you have
heard and do not add whatever
may be contrary nor subtract

both: While Barn agrees with H for this reading, ApCon renders the phrase differently as "for fear that they grumble about you and you experience God's anger"
(στενάξουσιν ἐπὶ σοὶ καὶ ἔσται σοι ὀργὴ παρὰ θεοῦ). For <God> does not come to
summon: ApCon omits the term "not" (οὐ), preferring a statement about human
responsibility and divine retribution here than what the reader might expect.
4.11 • And you slaves (ὑμεῖς δὲ οἱ δοῦλοι): H omits ὁ, which Bryennios emends
and most scholars include. ApCon offers the minor variant reading καὶ ὑμεῖς
οἱ δοῦλοι. Be obedient (ὑποτάγησεσθε): ApCon prefers the aorist imperative
ὑποτάγητε to the future passive of H here. To [your] masters: Bryennios emends
the text of H, which reads "to our (ἡμῶν) masters," to the present reading of "to
your" (ὑμῶν), as supported by ApCon and Doct (vestris). Most scholars follow
this emendation, though H may actually preserve the original reading.
4.12 • Does not please (μὴ ἀρεστὸν): H and Doct agree. Epit offers the verbal
variant μὴ ἀρέσκει with essentially the same meaning, and ApCon reads "if it
should not please" (ἐὰν ᾖ ἀρεστὸν). The Lord (τῷ κυρίῳ): ApCon and Epit read
with H here, though they omit the definite article. Barn and Doct read "God"
(θεοῦ; Doct=deo). At the close of the verse, ApCon (ποιήσεις) follows Doct (non
facies). This suggests a logical conclusion to the thought, though it is omitted by
H and Epit.
4.13 • But . . . what you have received (δὲ ἃ παρέλαβες): All texts agree here,
except Barn omits the "but" (δέ) and CO offers the slight variation ἅπερ ἔλαβες,
which likely reflects the editor's misreading of the exemplar. ApCon adds at
the conclusion "from him" (παρ᾽ αὐτοῦ) as a deduction from the logic of the
instruction. Neither adding nor subtracting: H reads here μήτε προστιθεὶς μήτε
ἀφαιρῶν, which CO renders "neither add nor diminish" (μήτε προσθείς μήτε
ὑφαιρῶν). ApCon adds the phrases "to them . . . from them" (ἀπ᾽ αὐτῶν) to each
verb respectively as logical completions of thought.†

4.11 All second person references in plural (as
with 1.3). *As exemplary of God* (ὡς τύπῳ θεοῦ): Lit.,
"in the place of God." Cf. IgnMag 6.1 (εἰς τόπον
θεοῦ) in reference to the role of the bishop. Cf.

Schöllgen 1991, 113.
4.12ff All second person references in singular
(as with 1.4–4.10).

[14]Disclose your wrongdoings in the community (ἐκκλησίᾳ) and do not approach your prayer with an evil conscience. This is the way of life.

5 But the way of death is this: first of all, it is evil and full of curses—murders, adulteries, lusts, depravities, thefts, idolatries, magical practices, potions, robberies, false testimonies, hypocrisies, deception, treachery, conceit, depravity, arrogance, greed, vulgarity, jealousy, haughtiness, loftiness, <and> boastfulness.

[2]<It includes> persecutors of good <folk>, who hate truth,

from it. [14]Do not approach prayer with an evil conscience. This is the way of life.

5 But the way of death is opposite to that: first, it is evil and full of curses—adulteries, murders, false testimonies, fornications, evil desires, magical practices, injurious potions, thefts, empty superstitions, robberies, hypocrisies, loathing, malice, impudence, covetousness, shameless talk, jealousy, haughtiness, pride, loftiness, <and> vanity.

[2]<It includes> audaciousness, persecuting good <folk>,

4.14 Cf. Jas 5:16;
1Jn 1:9
5.1 Cf. Mt 15:19

4.14 • In the community: This phrase appears in H only.† Wrongdoings (τὰ παραπτώματα): H and Epit support this reading, while Barn reads simply "because of sins" (ἐπὶ ἁμαρτίαις) and ApCon more elaborately "to the Lord God your sins" (κυρίῳ τῷ θεῷ σου τὰ ἁμαρτήματα). With an evil conscience (ἐν συνειδήσει πονηρᾷ): ApCon offers "in your day of evil" (ἐν ἡμέρᾳ πονηρίας σου), which presumably carries a similar meaning.
5.1 • But the way of death (ἡ δὲ τοῦ θανάτου ὁδός): ApCon reverses the elements "death" and "way" (ἡ δὲ ὁδὸς τοῦ θανάτου). Is this: first of all, it is evil and full of curses: Doct reads similarly (est illi contraria, primum nequam et maledictis plena), as does Barn with "is crooked and full of curses" (ἔστιν σκολιὰ καὶ κατάρας μεστή). ApCon offers "is seen in its evil practices" (ἐστὶν ἐν πράξεσιν πονηραῖς θεωρουμένη).† Lusts, depravities (ἐπιθυμίαι, πορνεῖαι): ApCon reads "depravities, perjuries, lusts, wrongdoings" (πορνεῖαι, ἐπιορκίαι, ἐπιθυμίαι, παράνομοι). Deception (διπλοκαρδία): Barn supports H. ApCon reads in the plural form διπλοκαρδίαι, reflecting the construction of those elements that immediately surround the term. Loftiness (ὕψος): Barn reads "loftiness of power" (ὕψος δυνάμεως), while ApCon offers the variant "being high minded" (ὑψηλοφροσύνη). Boastfulness (ἀλαζονεία): H and Geor agree on this reading. The term is followed in ApCon by "falsehood" (ἀφοβία) and in Doct by "audaciousness" (non timentes). The term is absent in Barn, which reads instead "lack of fear of God" (ἀφοβία θεοῦ).
5.2 • <It includes> persecutors . . . reward of righteousness: ApCon offers a variant reading that better concludes the list of 5.1 with "persecution of good <folk>, hate of truth, love of lies, ignorance of righteousness" (διωγμὸς ἀγαθῶν,

---

5.1 *Arrogance* (αὐθάδεια): Lit., "self will." Used often in classical Greek (Plato, Aristotle), the term

is found as well in Barn 20.1 and ApCon 7.18 as an illustration of traits that define the evil lifestyle.

6.1 Cf. Lv 15:13
6.2 Cf. Sir 51:26–27;
Mt 11:29–30

love a lie, do not recognize
the reward of righteousness,
do not cling to the good nor
evaluate truthfully, not keeping an eye out for good but
for evil, for whom modesty
and patience are far distant,
love useless things, chase after
compensation, do not show
mercy to the poor, do not work
for the victimized, do not
recognize the one who made
them, murder children, corrupt God's creation, turn away
the one in need, victimize the
oppressed, are intercessors for
the wealthy, dishonest judges
of the poor—altogether wicked.
Children, may you be kept safe
from all these things.

6 See that no one diverts
you from this way of teaching, since <that one> teaches
you with no concern for God.
²For if you can bear the whole
yoke of the Lord, you will be
satisfied. And if you cannot, do

hating truth, loving a lie, not
recognizing the reward of
truth, not clinging to the good,
not having unbiased judgment,
not keeping an eye out for
good but for evil, when gentle-
ness is distant and pride is
close, chasing after compensation, not showing mercy to the
poor, not being distressed for
the distressed, not recognizing
the creator, murdering their
children, procuring abortion,
turning away from a good
work, afflicting the oppressed,
<and> avoiding intercession
for the upright. Children, keep
yourselves safe from all these
things.

6 And see that no one diverts
you from this teaching; otherwise you will be instructed
outside the true discipline. ²If
you are mindful of this daily,
you will be near the living
God; if you do not do this, you

ἀληθείας ἔχθρα, ψεύδους ἀγάπη, ἄγνοια δικαιοσύνης). Do not cling to the good
(οὐ κολλώμενοι ἀγαθῷ): Doct reads similarly (non applicants se bonis), but Ap-
Con offers the broader rationale of "for those who do such things do not cling
to the good" (οἱ γὰρ τούτων ποιηταὶ οὐ κολλώμενοι ἀγαθῷ). Not keeping an eye
out (ἀγρυπνοῦντες οὐκ): While H uses the participial form, ApCon prefers simply
"do not keep an eye out" (ἀγρυπνοῦσιν οὐκ). The one in need . . . the oppressed:
H and Barn include the definite articles here, omitted by ApCon. Dishonest
judges (ἄνομοι κριταί): Barn reads with H. ApCon offers the variant "disdainers"
(ὑπερόπται).
6.1 • From this way of teaching . . . no concern for God: ApCon reads simply
"from godliness" (ἀπὸ τῆς εὐσεβείας). Doct reads slightly different with hac doctrina, et si minus extra disciplinam doceberis.†

6.2 *You will be satisfied* (τέλειος ἔσῃ): As with 1.4.

what you can. ³And regarding food, accept what you can; but certainly avoid what is offered to idols, for it is in service to dead gods.

will be far from truth. Keep all these things in mind and your hope will not be groundless. But by these holy struggles you will obtain a crown by the lord Jesus Christ, who reigns and rules with the Father and Holy Spirit for eternity. Amen.

6.3 Cf. Ac 15:29
7.1 Cf. Mt 28:19
7.3 Cf. Mt 28:19

7 And regarding baptism, baptize like this: having asserted all these things, baptize in the name of the Father and of the Son and of the Holy Spirit in running water. ²But if you do not have running water, baptize in some other <water>; and if you cannot <baptize> in cold water, <then baptize> in warm. ³But if you do not have either, pour water on the head three times in the name of Father and Son and Holy Spirit. ⁴And before the baptism, let the one who baptizes and the one who is to be baptized fast beforehand, as well as

---

6.3 • Food (βρώσεως): ApCon offers the plural form βρωμάτων. But certainly avoid what is offered to idols, for it is in service to dead gods: ApCon reads slightly different with "shun idols, for they sacrifice to them in honor of demons" (τῶν εἰδωλοθύτων φεύγετε· ἐπὶ τιμῇ γὰρ δαιμόνων θύουσιν ταῦτα).†
7.1 • Baptism: H includes the genitive singular form of the definite article (τοῦ), omitted by ApCon. Baptize like this: having asserted all these things, baptize: Geor follows H here. ApCon reads with ecclesiastical instruction, concluding with Matt 28:19–20: "oh bishop or presbyter . . . baptize like this, as the Lord commanded us, saying, 'Go, teach . . .'" (ὦ ἐπίσκοπε ἢ πρεσβύτερε . . . οὕτως βαπτίσεις, ὡς ὁ κύριος διετάξατο ἡμῖν λέγων· Πορευθέντες μαθητεύσατε . . .). In running water: Omitted by ApCon.†
7.2–3 • These verses are replaced by similar materials in ApCon, though much more oriented toward specific ecclesiastical instruction.

7.1ff All second person references in plural (as with 1.3 and 4.11).
7.2 *Running water*: Lit., "living water" (ὕδατι ζῶντι), that is, water that is moving and has not been sitting or stagnant, such as water in a cistern. *In cold water*: Presumably this is another indicator of the nature of living or running water as opposed to stagnant water, which has had time to be warmed by the sun.
7.3 *Father and Son and Holy Spirit*: Unlike 7.1, where this Trinitarian formula includes a definite article before each element (i.e., "the Father and the Son and the Holy Spirit"), the present phrase suggests that the formula is envisioned as a specific set of

names rather than labels of divinity. It is perhaps unexpected to find this diversity of expression in such closely related verses, but cf. JusAp 1.61 and AposTrad 21 (McDonald 1980, 191 n. 222).
7.4 *Let the one . . . fast beforehand* (προνηστευσάτω): Found in Herodotus and Hippocrates, this term is not used in ecclesiastical Greek literature. The LXX, NT, and ApCon use the more common terms νηστεύω and νηστεία. *As well as others who are able* (καὶ εἴ τινες ἄλλοι δύνανται): Presumably, this refers either to those who attend the baptism but are not being baptized themselves or who have assisted the baptismal candidate in the process.

8.1 Cf. Mt 6:16
8.2 Cf. ªMt 6:5
Cf. ᵇMt 6:9–13; Lk
11:2–4

others who are able. So too, instruct the one who is to be baptized to fast one or two <days> in advance.

8 And do not let your fasts be with the hypocrites, for they fast on the second and fifth <days> after the sabbath, but yourselves, you fast on the fourth <day> and day of preparation. ²And do not pray like the hypocrites but, as the Lord instructed in his gospel, pray as follows:

> Our Father who is in heaven,
> hallowed be your name,
> your kingdom come,
> your will be done on earth as it is in heaven.
> Give us this day our daily bread,
> and forgive us our debt as we forgive our debtors,
> and lead us not into temptation,
> but deliver us from evil,
> for yours are the power and the glory forever.

³Pray like this three times a day.

7.4 • Fast (προνηστευσάτω): ApCon reads with the variant form νηστευσάτω (Wengst 1984, 76). The one who baptizes . . . in advance: This concluding comment is omitted in ApCon, though alternate instructions for the baptismal candidate are included in its place.
8.1 • With the hypocrites: H and ApCon read together here. Eth prefers "as" (ὡς). You fast: H and Eth agree. ApCon offers "or you fast all five days or . . ." (ἢ πέντε νηστεύσατε ἡμέρας ἢ).†
8.2 • And do not pray like the hypocrites (μηδὲ προσεύχεσθε ὡς οἱ ὑποκριταί): H and Eth again agree, with ApCon reading "but when you pray, do not be like the hypocrites" (ὅταν δὲ προσεύχησθε, μὴ γίνεσθε ὥσπερ ὑποκριταί). The Lord instructed in his gospel (ἐκέλευσεν ὁ κύριος ἐν τῷ εὐαγγελίῳ αὐτοῦ): Eth agrees with H here, but follows the reading of ApCon, "the Lord commanded us in the gospel" (ὁ κύριος ἡμῖν ἐν τῷ εὐαγγελίῳ διετάξατο), when it omits "his" (αὐτοῦ). In heaven (ἐν τῷ οὐρανῷ): H reads the singular. ApCon offers the plural "in the heavens" (ἐν τοῖς οὐρανοῖς) in agreement with the manuscript tradition of Matt 6:9. On earth (ἐπὶ γῆς): ApCon adds "the" (ἐπὶ τῆς γῆς), which H omits. Our debt (τὴν ὀφειλὴν ἡμῶν): H again reads the singular. ApCon offers the plural "our debts" (τὰ ὀφειλήματα ἡμῶν) in agreement with Matt 6:12. For yours are the power (ὅτι σοῦ ἐστιν ἡ δύναμις): ApCon expands the closing formula with "for yours are the kingdom and the power . . ." (ὅτι σοῦ ἐστιν ἡ βασιλεία καὶ ἡ δύναμις). Forever: ApCon concludes the prayer with an "amen" (ἀμήν).

8.1 *Be with the hypocrites*: It is difficult to know whether this is a prohibition against fasting "with" the hypocrites or, instead, fasting "in the same manner as" the hypocrites. In either case, the Didachist reflects a certain rigidity here that is not otherwise typical of the text (McDonald 1980, 93; Draper 1992, 362–77). *Second and fifth . . . fourth <day> and day of preparation*: In contemporary

terms, this means Monday and Thursday versus Wednesday and Friday.
8.2 *Our Father who is in heaven*: This rendering of the Lord's prayer follows the traditional wording of Matthew, since the form is essentially the same. *From evil*: Or perhaps better, "from the evil one" (ἀπὸ τοῦ πονηροῦ).

9 And regarding the eucharist, give thanks like this: [2]First, regarding the cup:

> We thank you, our Father,
> for the holy vine your child (παιδός) David,
> whom you made known to us
> through your child (παιδός) Jesus—
> yours is the glory forever.

[3]And regarding the broken bread (κλάσματος):

> We thank you, our Father,
> for life and knowledge (γνώσεως),
> which you made known to us
> through your child (παιδός) Jesus—
> yours is the glory forever.

[4]Just as this broken bread (κλάσμα) was scattered over the hills
and, coming together, became one,
may your community (ἐκκλησία) likewise come together from
the ends of the earth into your kingdom—
for yours are the power and the glory through Jesus Christ
forever.

9.1 • And regarding: While H reads "and" (δέ), ApCon offers the minor variant μέν. Give thanks like this (οὕτως εὐχαριστήσατε): ApCon reads "thus saying" (οὕτως λέγοντες).
9.2 • First, regarding the cup: Omitted by ApCon. We thank you (εὐχαριστοῦμέν σοι): ApCon omits the term "you" (σοι) here. For the holy vine your child David . . . your child Jesus—yours . . . (ὑπὲρ τῆς ἁγίας ἀμπέλου Δαυὶδ τοῦ παιδός σου . . . σοὶ . . .): ApCon omits this phrase, and offers a much longer confessional statement framed by the words found in Did 9.3: "for that life you made known to us by Jesus your Son . . . for through him and . . ." (ὑπὲρ τῆς ζωῆς ἧς ἐγνώρισας ἡμῖν διὰ Ἰησοῦ τοῦ παιδός σου . . . δι᾽ αὐτοῦ γάρ σοι καὶ).† Forever: ApCon again concludes the prayer with an "amen" (ἀμήν).
9.3 • And regarding the broken bread: The term for "broken bread" (κλάσματος) found in H is unusual for the tradition. The more common word "bread" (ἄρτος) may have originally stood here in the Vorlage (Wengst 1984, 78; Peterson 1959, 146–82). ApCon omits the phrase altogether. And knowledge: Omitted by ApCon. Yours is the glory forever: Omitted by ApCon.
9.4 • Broken bread: Omitted by ApCon. Over the hills: Omitted by ApCon. Became one (ἐγένετο ἕν): ApCon reads "became one loaf" (ἐγένετο εἷς ἄρτος). May your community likewise come together (οὕτως συναχθήτω σου ἡ ἐκκλησία): ApCon offers "may the church likewise come together" (οὕτως συνάγαγέ σου τὴν

9.2 *Child . . . child*: This term may be translated either as "servant" or "child," but may here reflect a conscious play in concept on the part of the author.
9.4 *Was scattered over the hills and, coming together, became one*: The meaning of this phrase is not

immediately obvious, but may suggest "as the seed was sown and then was gathered to make the bread." Scholarly debate ranges widely here.

9.5 Cf. Mt 7:6a
10.2 Cf. ᵃJn 17:11
Cf. ᵇLk 1:49; Mt 6:9;
Lk 11:2
10.3 Cf. Wis 1:14; Sir
18:1; 3Mc 2:9; Rv 4:11

⁵And no one shall eat or drink from your eucharist except those who are baptized in the Lord's name, for the Lord has also spoken about this: "Do not give what is holy to dogs."

10 And after being filled, give thanks as follows: ²We thank you, holy Father, for your holy name that you caused to inhabit [our] hearts, and for the knowledge (γνώσεως) and faith and immortality that you made known to us through your child (παιδός) Jesus— yours is the glory forever. ³You yourself, all-powerful Master, created all things for your name's sake, and

[Coptic (*Brit.Lib.Or.Mus.* 9271)]

ἐκκλησίαν), reflecting an ecclesiastical consciousness that is more institutional in scope. For yours are the power and the glory through Jesus Christ forever: Omitted by ApCon.†

9.5 • Shall eat or drink . . . holy to dogs: ApCon reads differently with "eat of these things who are uninitiated, but only those who are baptized into the Lord's death" (ἐσθιέτω ἐξ αὐτῶν τῶν ἀμυήτων, ἀλλὰ μόνοι οἱ βεβαπτισμένοι εἰς τὸν τοῦ κυρίου θάνατον).†

10.1 • Being filled (τὸ ἐμπλησθῆναι): ApCon reads "the communion" (τὴν μετάληψιν), perhaps to symbolize the liturgical significance of the meal in the sense of an ecclesiastical Eucharist rather than merely as a deipnon event.

10.2 • We thank (εὐχαριστοῦμέν) you: H and ApCon agree on the plural form of the verb against Geor's singular reading of "I thank you" (εὐχαριστῶ). Holy Father: ApCon offers "God and Father of Jesus our Savior" (ὁ θεὸς καὶ πατὴρ Ἰησοῦ τοῦ σωτῆρος ἡμῶν). To inhabit [our] hearts (ἐν ταῖς καρδίαις ἡμῶν): ApCon offers "in us" (ἐν ἡμῖν). The possessive "our" is an emendation by Bryennios, since H reads "your" (ὑμῶν), which is a likely error in the manuscript (Wengst 1984, 80). Hearts: Geor continues the next stanza with a repetition of the phrase "I thank you." Faith: ApCon adds after this "and love" (καὶ ἀγάπης). You made known to us (ἐγνώρισας ἡμῖν): Geor omits "to us" (ἡμῖν), while ApCon offers "you gave to us" (ἔδωκας ἡμῖν). Yours is the glory forever: Omitted by ApCon.

10.3 • All-powerful Master: ApCon adds "God of the universe" (ὁ θεὸς τῶν ὅλων). All things for your name's sake . . . so that they might thank you: While Copt reads similarly, ApCon offers "the world and the things in it by him, and planted law within us, and before that prepared things for human convenience" (τὸν κόσμον καὶ τὰ ἐν αὐτῷ δι' αὐτοῦ, καὶ νόμον κατεφύτευσας ἐν ταῖς ψυχαῖς ἡμῶν καὶ τὰ πρὸς μετάληψιν προευτρέπισας ἀνθρώποις). To humanity (ἀνθρώποις): H and ApCon agree on this word. Copt offers the extended phrase "children of humanity" (ϣⲏⲣⲓ ⲛ̄ⲛⲣⲱⲙⲓ) to indicate the same idea. So that they might thank you: Both ApCon and Copt omit this phrase. But you favored us: Copt adds the phrase "you gave us" (ⲉⲁⲕⲧ ⲛⲉⲛ). ApCon omits the text of H from gave food and drink to humanity to enjoy so that they might thank you.

But you favored us with spiritual food and drink, and eternal life through your child (παιδός σου).
⁴In particular, we thank you that you yourself are mighty—yours is the glory forever.

⁵Remember your community (ἐκκλησία), Lord, to shield it from all evil and to perfect it in your love, and, being made holy, bring it together from the four winds into your kingdom, which you made ready for it—for yours are the power and the glory forever.

³. . . and gave them to the children of humanity for enjoyment.

But <as for> us, you favored us, you gave us spiritual food and drink, and eternal life through Jesus your son (ⲡⲉⲕϣⲏⲣⲓ).
⁴We thank you for all things because you are mighty—yours is the glory forever. Amen.

⁵Remember your community (ⲉⲕⲗⲏⲥⲓⲁ), Lord, to rescue it from all evil, and you make it perfect by your love, that you bring it together from the four winds into your kingdom, which you made ready for it—for yours are the power and the glory forever. Amen.

10.5 Cf. ᵃMt 6:13
Cf. ᵇJn 17:23; 1Jn 4:12
Cf. ᶜMt 24:31; Zech 2:10

this phrase through the end of 10.4. Through your child (διὰ τοῦ παιδός σου): H and ApCon agree with this reading. Copt reads "through Jesus your son" (ⲉⲃⲁⲗ ϩⲓⲧⲛ ⲓ̅ⲏ̅ⲥ̅ ⲡⲉⲕϣⲏⲣⲓ), as does Geor (διὰ Ἰησοῦ τοῦ παιδός σου).
10.4 • In particular (πρὸ πάντων): Lit., "above all things." Copt renders this phrase as "for all things" (ⲉⲧⲃⲉ ϩⲱⲃ ⲛⲓⲃⲓ). You yourself (εἶ σύ): Copt and Geor omit the nominative pronoun σύ, which is used to intensify the subject. Are mighty: Geor adds "and good" (καὶ ἀγαθός). Yours is the glory forever: Copt adds a concluding "amen" (ϩⲁⲙⲏⲛ).
10.5 • Lord: H and Copt agree on this reading, though it is omitted by ApCon. Your community . . . to shield it (τῆς ἐκκλησίας σου, τοῦ ῥύσασθαι αὐτὴν): H and Copt read similarly here. ApCon diverges, reading "your holy church, which you bought through the precious blood of your Christ, and shield it" (τῆς ἁγίας σου ἐκκλησίας ταύτης, ἣν περιεποιήσω τῷ τιμίῳ αἵματι τοῦ Χριστοῦ σου, καὶ ῥῦσαι αὐτὴν). In your love: H and Copt read similarly, while ApCon adds "and your truth" (καὶ τῇ ἀληθείᾳ σου). Perfect (τελειῶσαι): H and Copt read similarly, while ApCon omits the term. Bring it together from the four winds (σύναξον αὐτὴν ἀπὸ τεσσάρων ἀνέμων): H and Copt again agree; ApCon reads "gather us all together" (συνάγαγε πάντας ἡμᾶς). Being made holy (τὴν ἁγιασθεῖσαν): H and Geor agree on this reading. Both Copt and ApCon omit the phrase. Made ready for it (αὐτῇ): H, Copt, and ApCon all favor the feminine singular dative form of the pronoun "it" as a reference to "kingdom." Geor uses the masculine singular dative αὐτῷ, which is surely a mistake, since there is no obvious antecedent for this form. For yours are the power and the glory forever: Omitted by ApCon. Copt again adds a concluding "amen."

10.6 Cf. ᵃMt 21:9, 15
Cf. ᵇ1Cor 16:22
11.1–2 Cf. Mt 5:17,
19–20

⁶Let grace come and this world come to an end!

Hosanna to the God of David!

If anyone is holy, let them come;

if anyone is not, let them repent!

The Lord come (μαραναθά)! Amen.

⁷But allow the prophets to give thanks as they wish.

11 As a result, if someone who comes should teach you all that has been asserted here,

⁶Let the Lord come and this world come to an end! Amen.

Hosanna to the house of David!

The one who is holy, let them come;

the one who is not holy, let them repent!

The Lord has come! Amen.

⁷But allow the prophets to give thanks as they wish. But concerning the saying for the ointment, give thanks as you say:

We thank you, Father, for the ointment that you showed us through Jesus your son (пекаϭнрι)—yours is the glory forever. Amen.

11 As a result, that one who comes and teaches you these things that we have said, ac-

10.6 • Let grace come and this world come to an end: Omitted by ApCon. Grace (χάρις): Copt reads "the Lord" (п̄х̄с̄). Come to an end: Copt again adds a concluding "amen." God (θεῷ): ApCon reads "son" (υἱῷ); Copt offers "house" (нⲓ). Is holy, let them come (ἅγιός ἐστιν, ἐρχέχθω): ApCon offers the slight variant ἅγιός, προσερχέσθω. If anyone is not: ApCon adds the adversative "but" (δέ) to form the phrase "but if anyone is not." Let them repent! The Lord come! Amen: H and Copt basically agree. ApCon offers "let them be <such> by repenting" (γινέσθω διὰ μετανοίας).

10.7 • But allow the prophets to give thanks as they wish: Copt reads similarly to H. ApCon has instead "but also permit your prophets to give thanks" (ἐπιτρέπετε δὲ καὶ τοῖς πρεσβυτέροις ὑμῶν εὐχαροστεῖν). As they wish (ὅσα θέλουσιν): Copt offers a similar construction with н̄ⲟн ⲉⲧⲉϩнⲉⲩ, while Geor reads "to God as they wish" (θεῷ ὅσα θέλουσιν).†

11.1 • As a result . . . accept them: H and Copt roughly agree here. ApCon offers "if someone who comes should give thanks like this, receive them as a disciple of Christ" (ὃς ἐὰν ἐλθὼν οὕτως εὐχαριστῇ, προσδέξασθε αὐτὸν ὡς Χριστοῦ μαθητήν). Teach you all (πάντα): Copt omits "all." Accept them: Copt adds "among yourselves" (ϣⲁⲡϥ ⲉⲣⲁⲧⲉн).

11.1ff All second person references in plural.

accept them. ²But if the one who teaches should change <so as> to teach another teaching that is destructive, do not listen to them. Then again, to the degree that it provides righteousness and knowledge of the Lord, accept them as Lord. ³But regarding the apostles and prophets, proceed like this in agreement with the decree (δόγμα) of the gospel: ⁴And every apostle who comes to you, accept them as Lord. ⁵And they should not stay <except>

cept them among yourselves. ²But if the one who teaches should change and teach you another <teaching>, destroying the first, do not listen to them. But if that one should provide righteousness and knowledge of the Lord, accept them among yourselves as the Lord. ³But regarding the apostles and prophets, proceed according to the word (ⲡⲥⲉϫⲓ) of the gospel as follows: ⁴Every apostle who comes to you, ⁵let them stay a day. But if there is a need,

11.2 Cf. 2Jn 10

11.2 • But if the one who teaches . . . do not listen to them: H and Copt roughly agree here, with ApCon reading alternatively, "but if someone preaches another teaching apart from what Christ gave to you through us, do not let this one give thanks" (ἐὰν δὲ ἄλλην διδαχὴν κηρύσσῃ παρ᾽ ἣν ὑμῖν παρέδωκεν ὁ Χριστὸς δι᾽ ἡμῶν, τῷ τοιούτῳ μὴ συγχωρεῖτε εὐχαριστεῖν).† That is destructive (εἰς τὸ καταλῦσαι): Copt offers "destroying the first" (ⲉϥⲃⲱⲗ ⲉⲃⲁⲗ ⲛ̄ⲡⲓϩⲟⲩⲉϯ) in reference to the original words of teaching. Geor adds "of the things said before" (τὰ προειρημένα). Do not listen to them: Lit., "to him" (αὐτοῦ). ApCon reads "this one" (τῷ τοιούτῳ). Then again . . . accept them as Lord: Omitted by ApCon. Accept them: Copt adds the phrase "among yourselves" (ⲉⲗⲁⲧⲉⲛ).
11.3 • Decree (δόγμα): Both H and Eth agree. Copt uses the less ecclesiastical term "word" (ⲡⲥⲉϫⲓ). ApCon omits the entire verse.
11.4 • And (δέ) every apostle: Eth omits the conjunction. Receive as Lord: Both ApCon and Eth omit this phrase.
11.5 • And they should not stay <except> (οὐ μενεῖ δὲ εἰ μή): Emended from Eth. Copt reads "let them stay" (ⲙⲁⲣⲉϥϭⲱ). One day: Eth adds "or another" (ἢ τὴν ἄλλην). But if: Both H and Copt support the adversative reading "but" (δέ). Eth

---

11.2 *To the degree that it provides righteousness and knowledge of the Lord:* The meaning of the articular infinitive (εἰς τὸ προσθεῖναι) is unclear. Translators typically read this to indicate some distinction between the destructive teaching (or teacher) mentioned in the previous instruction of 11.2 and that which (or who), in contrast, offers righteousness and knowledge. On the other hand, this may suggest instead that, even if the teaching itself is destructive and should be avoided, at least "for the sake of righteousness and knowledge of the Lord" the teacher should be received "as Lord" according to the customs of ancient hospitality.
11.3 *In agreement with the decree of the gospel:* It is

uncertain here whether "gospel" (εὐαγγέλιον) indicates some sort of "gospel tradition" (cf. Köster 1957, 159–241) or, instead, a specific written gospel that was known to the author (cf. Massaux 1950, 604–46; Wengst 1984, 24–32). If the latter, then this is our earliest such reference in literature.
11.5 *And they should not stay <except> one day.* The word "except" is a logical completion of the intended idea and, based on Eth, is included in the translation here. Copt provides the instruction in a positive tone, which may reflect the intention of the author and explain the confusion behind the alternative renderings of the manuscript traditions.

11.7 Cf. Mt 12:31
11.8 Cf. Mt 7:15–23

one day; but if there is a need, then another <day>. But if they stay three <days>, they are a false prophet. ⁶And when the apostle goes, they are to accept nothing except food (ἄρτον) until they can find a place to stay; but if they should ask for money (ἀργύριον), they are a false prophet. ⁷And neither test nor judge any prophet who speaks in a spirit. For every sin will be forgiven, but this sin will not be forgiven. ⁸But not everyone who speaks in a spirit is a prophet, but <only> if they have the Lord's traits. So it is by such traits that the

let them stay two days. But if they stay three days, they are a false prophet. ⁶And when the apostle goes away, they are to take nothing except a fragment (ⲗⲁⲡϯ) until they rest. But if they should take money (ⲉⲁⲙⲛⲧ), they are a false prophet. ⁷Any prophet who speaks in a spirit, neither test nor judge them. For every sin will be forgiven you, but this sin will not be forgiven you. ⁸Not everyone who speaks in a spirit is prophetic (ⲉⲉⲛ ⲡⲣⲟⲫⲏⲧⲏⲥ), but if the ways of the Lord are with them. Thus, by these ways you shall know the prophet

prefers "and" (καί). Then another (καὶ τὴν ἄλλην): Having provided this phrase previously, Eth reads here "and a third" (καὶ τὴν τρίτην). Copt reads "two days" (ⲛ̄ⲉⲁⲟⲩ ⲃ̄). But if they stay three (τρεῖς δὲ ἐὰν μείνῃ): Copt adds "days" (ⲛ̄ⲉⲁⲟⲩ) as the logical completion of the idea, included in the translation here. Eth reads "but if they stay more" (περισσότερον δὲ ἐὰν μείνῃ).
11.6 • Ask for money: H uses the term "ask" (αἰτῇ), while Copt has "take" (ⲁϥϣⲁⲛⲭⲓ).†
11.7 • And neither test: Both H and Eth use "here" (καί) at this juncture, which Copt omits. Neither test . . . speaks in a spirit: H and Copt roughly agree on this reading. Eth offers "each prophet who speaks in a spirit shall be tested and judged so that there may be no sin" (πᾶς προφήτης λαλῶν ἐν πνεύματι πειρασθήτω καὶ διακριθήτω, ἵνα μὴ ἁμαρτία τι ᾖ). Nor judge: Copt adds "them" (ⲉⲧⲃⲏⲧϥ̄; lit., "concerning him"). In a spirit: H, Copt, and Eth agree on this reading. Geor reads "in a holy spirit" (ἐν πνεύματι ἁγίῳ). For every sin . . . will not be forgiven: Omitted by Eth. For every sin will be forgiven: Copt adds "you" (ⲛⲏⲧⲛ). Will not be forgiven: Copt again adds "you."†
11.8 • But not everyone (οὐ πᾶς δὲ): Copt omits the adversative "but" (δέ), while Eth reads "and everyone" (καὶ πᾶς). In a spirit: H, Copt, and Eth agree. Geor again reads "in a holy spirit" (ἐν πνεύματι ἁγίῳ). But <only> if (ἀλλ᾽ ἐὰν): Eth omits "but" (ἀλλά). The Lord's traits (τοὺς τρόπους κυρίου): Copt reads similarly. Eth offers "the traits of God" (τοὺς τρόπους τοῦ θεοῦ).† So it is by such traits: Copt reads similarly to H. Eth begins with "a true prophet is" (προφήτης ἀληθινός ἐστιν). The false prophet can be distinguished from the prophet: The wording of Copt is not as complex, and some scholars think this represents the original (Wengst 1984, 84). Geor adds "true" (ἀληθινός) to "the prophet" in order to provide the obvious parallel with "false prophet." Eth reads "each (πᾶς) false prophet or <true> prophet can be distinguished."

false prophet can be distinguished from the prophet. ⁹And each prophet who arranges for food in a spirit must not eat it. Otherwise, they are a false prophet. ¹⁰And each prophet who teaches the truth, if they do not do what they teach, is a false prophet. ¹¹But any prophet, having been confirmed as true, who enacts a worldly mystery on behalf of the assembly (ἐκκλησίας)— even if not teaching <others> to act the same—let them not be judged by you, for it is God's decision. Even the early prophets acted in the same way. ¹²And anyone who says in the spirit, "Give me money (ἀργύρια)" or something else,

who is true. ⁹Each prophet who arranges for food yet does not eat it is a false prophet in this regard. ¹⁰And every prophet who teaches in truth yet does not do it is a false prophet. ¹¹Every prophet, having truly been confirmed, who teaches and expresses a worldly tradition in the assembly—let them not be judged by you, but judgment of them is with God. Thus the prophets did also in <their> time. ¹²And anyone who says in a spirit, "Give me some money (ϩⲉⲛϩⲁⲙⲧ)" or something else, do not listen to them. But if they should say it to you for others in need, let none of you judge them.

11.9 • In a spirit: H and Eth agree on this reading, which Copt omits.† Must not eat it (εἰ δὲ μήγε): H and Eth agree, while Copt offers "yet does not eat it" (ⲉⲛϥⲟⲩⲱⲙ ⲉⲃⲁⲗ ⲛ̅ϩⲏⲧⲥ).
11.10 • And each (πᾶς δὲ): Copt reads "and every" (ⲡⲉ ⲁⲅⲱ). The truth: H and Copt read similarly. Eth omits the phrase. If they do not do what they teach (εἰ ἃ διδάσκει οὐ ποιεῖ): Copt offers the slightly different "yet does not do it" (ⲉⲛϥⲓⲣⲓ ⲙⲁⲥ), while Eth offers "and does not act in truth" (καὶ οὐ ποιῶν ἀληθῶς).
11.11 • And any prophet: Eth follows H here. Copt omits "and" (δέ). Having been confirmed as true (δεδοκιμασμένος ἀληθινός): Eth again follows H. Copt reads "having truly been confirmed" (ⲉⲁⲩⲉⲣ ⲉϩⲁⲩⲉⲣⲇⲟⲕⲓⲙⲁⲍⲉⲓⲛ ⲙ̅ⲙⲁϥ). Who enacts a worldly mystery . . . to act the same: Copt reads "who teaches and expresses a worldly tradition in the assembly" (ⲉϥ†ⲥⲃⲱ ⲁⲅⲱ ⲉϥⲉⲣⲙⲉⲧⲣⲏ ⲛⲛⲟⲩⲡⲁⲣⲁⲇⲱⲥⲓⲥ ⲛ̅ⲕⲱⲥⲙⲉⲓⲕⲱⲛ ϩⲛ ⲧⲉⲕ'ⲕⲗⲏⲥⲓⲁ). Eth has "who acts unlawfully in the church like improper people" (ποιῶν ἐν ἐκκλησίᾳ ἀνθρώπων καὶ ποιῶν ἀνόμως).† For it is God's decision (μετὰ θεοῦ γὰρ ἔχει τὴν κρίσιν): Copt offers the adversative "but" (ἀλλά) in the place of the "for" (γάρ) found in H and Eth. Even the early prophets: H offers the reading γάρ . . . καί (translated here as "even"), while Copt omits "for" (γάρ) and Eth omits "and" (καί).

11.11 *A worldly mystery on behalf of the assembly:* This is a difficult phrase (εἰς μυστήριον κοσμικὸν ἐκκλησίας) to construe, since the author suggests that an approved prophet can somehow be found to be acting in a manner contrary to what might be expected in the assembly yet not teaching others to imitate the same. The nature of that activity

is not further defined. The Coptic text is defective here, but seems to offer the alternative "a worldly tradition in the assembly" (ⲛⲕⲟⲩⲡⲁⲣⲁⲇⲱⲥⲓⲥ ⲛⲕⲱⲥⲙⲉⲓⲕⲱⲛ ϩⲛ ⲧⲉⲕⲕⲗⲏⲥⲓⲁ). *For it is God's decision:* Lit., "for with God is the judgment" (μετὰ θεοῦ γὰρ ἔχει τὴν κρίσιν).

12.1 Cf. Ps 118:26 (LXX=117:26); Mt 21:9; Rm 12:13

do not listen to them. But if they should ask from you on behalf of others who are in need, let no one judge them.

12 And anyone who comes in the name of the Lord shall be welcomed. But inspecting them next, you will know, for you [will] have understanding <of the> true and false. ²If the one who comes is a traveler (παρόδιός), assist them as you are able. But they shall not remain with you for more than two or three days if necessary.

12 And everyone who comes to you in the name of the Lord, you shall receive them. But examine them and discern them, <for> you yourselves know the true and false. ²And if someone comes to you from the road, assist them.

11.12 • They should ask (εἴπη δοῦναι): H and Eth agree on this reading. Copt reads "they should say it to you" (ⲁϥϣⲁⲛⲭⲁⲁⲥ ⲛⲏⲧⲛ). This phrase follows the next ("of others who are in need") in the structure of the text. Of others who are in need (περὶ ἄλλων ὑστερούντων): Copt reads more simply "for others in need" (ⲉⲧⲃⲉ ⲅⲁ͞ⲓⲛⲓ ⲉⲩϣⲁⲣⲉ), while Eth offers only "of another" (περὶ ἄλλου). No one (μηδείς): H and Eth agree, while Copt offers a negative causal imperative form translated here as "none of you" (ⲙ̄ⲡⲉⲣⲧⲉ).
12.1 • Who comes (ὁ ἐρχόμενος): While this is the reading in H, the additional phrase "to you" (πρὸς ὑμᾶς) is preferred by ApCon, Copt, Eth, and Geor. In the name of the Lord (ἐν ὀνόματι κυρίου): H and Copt agree on this wording, while it is omitted by ApCon. Eth concludes with "of us" (ἡμῶν). Shall be welcomed . . . you will know: H and Eth agree. ApCon reverses the initial elements to "shall be inspected and then welcomed" (δοκιμασθείς, οὕτως δεχέσθω). Copt offers "you shall receive them. But examine them and discern them" (ϣⲁⲡⲟⲩ ⲉⲣⲁⲧⲛ ⲛ̄ⲧⲁⲧ͞ⲛ ⲇⲉ ⲇⲱⲕⲉⲓⲙⲁⲍⲉⲓⲛ ⲙⲁϥ). For you [will] have understanding: H, ApCon, and Eth agree on "for" (γάρ), while Copt omits it.† You [will] have (ἕξετε): Bryennios emends the Greek of H here from ἕξεται, which he considers to be an iotacism. Eth uses the present tense "you have" (ἔχετε). Copt reads "you yourselves know" (ⲟⲩⲛ̄ⲧⲏⲧⲛ ⲙⲉⲅ ⲣⲱⲧⲛ ⲛⲟⲩⲉⲓⲙⲉⲓ); ApCon combines the verbs to read "you have and are able to know" (ἔχετε καὶ δύνασθε γνῶναι).
12.2 • If (εἰ μὲν): This is the form offered by H, while an adversative conjunction is used by Copt (ⲇⲉ) and Eth (εἰ δέ). The one who comes: The phrase "to you" is added by Copt (ϣⲁⲣⲁⲧⲛ) and Geor (πρὸς ὑμᾶς), while Eth drops the clause altogether. Three days if necessary. And if they want (ἡμέρας ἐὰν ἦ ἀνάγκη. εἰ δὲ θέλει): Eth reads "three days; but if necessary and they want" (ἡμέρας· ἐὰν δὲ ἦ ἀνάγκη καὶ θέλη).

12.1 *<Of the> true and false*: Lit., "<of the> right and left" (δειξιὰν καὶ ἀριστερὰν).
12.2 *Traveler* (παρόδιος): Used by Hyperides in the fourth century BCE to mean "on the street," ultimately coming to mean "common" or "typi-

cal." The classical term for "traveler" is παροδίτης. The LXX uses πάροδος similarly, and in 1 Cor 16:7 the term is employed to mean "in passing" (Schaff 1885, 103).

³And if they want to settle among you <and> are a worker (τεχνίτης), let them work and eat. ⁴But if they are not a worker, decide through your own insight how they shall live among you as an active Christian. ⁵And if they do not want to cooperate like this, they are a Christ peddler. Watch out for these types!

13 And any true prophet who wants to stay with you is worthy of their share. ²A true prophet, like a worker, is likewise worthy of their share. ³So taking all the first yield of the wine press and threshing floor, and of the cattle and sheep, give <them> to the prophets, for

12.4 Cf. 2Th 3:7–12
13.1 Cf. Mt 10:10;
Luke 10:7; 1Cor
9:13–14; 1 Tm 5:18
13.3 Cf. Sir 7:29–31;
Mt 10:10

12.3 • And eat: Eth reads "and if they do not work, let them not eat" (εἰ δὲ οὐκ ἐργάζει, μὴ φαγέτω).
12.4 • Are not a worker: Eth adds "and do not work" (καὶ οὐκ ἐργάζει). As an active Christian (ζήσεται Χριστιανός): Eth reads "shall remain" (μενεῖ).
12.5 • Watch out: Eth begins the phrase with "and" (καί).
13.1 • And any (πᾶς δὲ): ApCon omits "and" (δέ), while Eth offers "therefore" (οὖν) in its place. True prophet who wants to stay with you (προφήτης ἀληθινὸς θέλων καθῆσθαι πρὸς ὑμᾶς): Eth agrees with H. ApCon reads "true prophet or teacher who comes to you" (προφήτης ἀληθινὸς ἢ διδάσκαλος ἐρχόμενος πρὸς ὑμᾶς). Of their share (τῆς τροφῆς αὐτοῦ): ApCon reads "of a share as a worker of the righteous word" (τῆς τροφῆς ὡς ἐργάτης λόγου δικαιοσύνης).
13.2 • A true prophet . . . of their share: This verse is missing altogether in both Eth and ApCon, though ApCon preserves its structure partially in the previous verse. The manuscripts for ApCon are not in agreement here.
13.3 • So (οὖν): H and Eth agree on this reading, though it is missing in ApCon. Taking (λαβών): This term is missing in both ApCon and Eth. It appears after the phrase "of the cattle and sheep," and thus is out of sequence here with respect to

12.4 *As an active Christian*: Lit., "not idle . . . Christian" (μὴ ἀργὸς . . . Χριστιανός).
12.5 *Christ peddler*: This term first appears here within Christian literature (cf. its appearance again with fourth-century authors Athanasius, Basil, Gregory Nazianzus, and Chrysostom), presumably with the meaning of someone who makes a living by means of their association with

the name of Christ.
13.3 *Give <them>*: The word "them" is inserted *ad sensum* for the purpose of translation in order not to repeat "first yield" (ἀπαρχή), which appeared earlier in the verse. Both H and Eth agree that the term is repeated. ApCon and Geor omit it, as does the translation here.

13.5 Cf. Nm 15:20–21

they are your high priests. [4]And when you have no prophet, give <them> to the poor. [5]When you make bread, take the first <batch and> give according to the instruction (ἐντολήν). [6]When you likewise open a container of wine or oil, take the first <measure and> give <it> to the prophets. [7]And money and clothing and any possessions, take the best as seems right to you <and> give according to the instruction (ἐντολήν).

14 When you come together on the Lord's day <and> after having acknowledged your offenses so that [your] sacrifice may be

the wording of the manuscript. And threshing floor: Both H and Eth support the presence of "and" (καί), while it is omitted by ApCon. First yield (τὴν ἀπαρχὴν): H, ApCon, and Eth agree on this reading, omitted by Geor. To the prophets (τοῖς προφήταις): While H and Eth agree on this reading, ApCon prefers "to the priests" (τοῖς ἱερεῦσιν). Geor offers "to the speakers of God" or "to the theologians" (τοῖς θεολόγοις). For they are your high priests: ApCon omits this clause.†
13.4 • And when you have no prophet, give <them> to the poor. Eth generally follows H here. ApCon reads "give a tenth of all to the orphan and the widow, the poor and the stranger" (πᾶσαν δεκάτην δώσεις τῷ ὀρφανῷ καὶ τῇ χήρᾳ, τῷ πτωχῷ καὶ τῷ προσηλύτῳ). To the poor: H reads with the plural τοῖς πτωχοῖς, while ApCon and Eth offer the singular τῷ πτωχῷ.
13.5 • when you make bread . . . according to the instruction: ApCon and Geor omit this verse. when you make bread: Eth begins with "and" (καί). Take the first: Eth omits the participle "taking" (λαβών), translated here as "take."
13.6 • When you likewise open a container: H and Eth begin literally with "likewise, a container . . ." (ὡσαύτως κεράμιον), while ApCon reads, "all the yield of hot bread, of a container" (πᾶσαν ἀπαρχὴν ἄρτων θερμῶν, κεραμίου). Wine or oil: Eth reads "and honey" (καὶ μέλιτος), while ApCon reads further with "or honey, or nuts, grapes or other things" (ἢ μέλιτος ἢ ἀκροδρύων, σταφυλῆς ἢ τῶν ἄλλων). Take: ApCon omits the participle "taking" (λαβών), translated here as "take." Eth reads with H. Give (δός): H and Eth offer the aorist here. ApCon prefers the future δώσεις. To the prophets (τοῖς προφήταις): ApCon prefers "to the priests" (τοῖς ἱερεῦσιν) as with 13.3, while Eth reads "to the poor" (τοῖς πτωχοῖς) as with 13.4.
13.7 • Take the best . . . according to the instruction: Eth adds "of the Lord" (τοῦ κυρίου); ApCon reads "to the orphan and the widow" (τῷ ὀρφανῷ καὶ τῇ χήρᾳ) as with 13.4.
14.1 • When you come together . . . and give thanks: ApCon reads similarly, with minor variations.† On the Lord's day (κατὰ κυριακὴν . . . κυρίου): ApCon reads "on the . . . day of the Lord, the Lord's day" (τὴν . . . τοῦ κυρίου ἡμέραν, τὴν κυριακήν). Geor offers simply "on the day" (καθ' ἡμέραν). [Your] sacrifice (ἡ θυσία ὑμῶν): This emendation by Bryennios is supported by ApCon and Geor. H

13.5 *Make bread*: The term σιτία, translated here as "bread," literally means "a batch of bread." Classical literature, LXX, the NT, and later patristic authors all use σιτίον and σῖτος ("grain"), as well as ἄρτος ("bread").
14.1 *On the Lord's day*: Lit., "Lord's day of the Lord"

(κυριακὴν . . . κυρίου). This is a difficult phrase that finds an abbreviated parallel ("Lord's day" [κυριακή]) in Rev 1:10 and IgnMag 9.1. The reference is presumably to that day of the week when Christians worshipped (i.e., Sunday) rather than to an annual event. Cf. 1 Cor 11:20. *Having acknowl-*

pure, break bread and give thanks. ²But nobody who has a dispute
with their friend should meet with you until they have made peace,
so that [your] sacrifice not become impure. ³For this is that about
which the Lord said, "In every place and time offer me a pure sacrifice, because I am a great king, says the Lord, and my name is
marvelous among the nations."

14.2 Cf. Mt 5:23–24
14.3 Cf. Mal 1:11, 14

15 So appoint bishops and deacons for yourselves who are worthy of the Lord, humble and modest and true men who have been
inspected, for they serve you as those <who implement> the minis-
try of the prophets and teachers. ²Do not disrespect them, for they
represent your integrity <in the same way as do> the prophets and

reads "our" (ἡμῶν). With respect to the structure of the text, this phrase comes
at the end of the verse after "pure." Pure (καθαρά): ApCon reads "faultless"
(ἄμεμπτος).
14.2 • But nobody who has . . . your sacrifice not become impure: ApCon omits
the entire verse. [Your] sacrifice (ἡ θυσία ὑμῶν): This emendation by Bryennios
is again supported by ApCon and Geor. H reads "our" (ἡμῶν).
14.3 • For this is that about which the Lord said: ApCon reads "to God, who said
concerning his universal church" (θεῷ, τῷ εἰπόντι περὶ τῆς οἰκουμενικῆς αὐτοῦ
ἐκκλησίας). Offer me a pure sacrifice: ApCon prefers "incense and pure sacrifice
shall be offered to me" (μοι προσενεχθήσεται θυμίαμα καὶ θυσία καθαρά). Because I am a great king: ApCon inserts the pronoun "I" (ἐγώ) to make the reading
subject specific: "because I myself am a great king." Says the Lord: ApCon adds
"all-powerful Master" (παντοκράτωρ), a term that appears in the Didache only
at 10.3, where it is further emended by ApCon with "God of the universe" (ὁ θεὸς
τῶν ὅλων).
15.1 • So appoint . . . worthy of the Lord: ApCon reads with slight (though
significant) alteration here, "but appoint bishops worthy of the Lord, and
presbyters and deacons" (προχειρίσασθε δὲ ἐπισκόπους ἀξίους τοῦ κυρίου καὶ
πρεσβυτέρους καὶ διακόνους).† Humble and modest . . . have been inspected:
ApCon offers a more expanded description with "pious, righteous, meek, lovers
of truth, free from love of money, who have been inspected, holy . . ." (εὐλαβεῖς,
δισαίους, πραεῖς, ἀφιλαργύρους, φιλαλήθεις, δεδοκιμασμένους, ὁσίους . . .). For
they serve . . . the prophets and teachers: ApCon omits this clause.
15.2 • Do not disrespect them . . . prophets and teachers: ApCon does not contain these words, but reads "and you yourselves honor these as fathers, lords,

edged (προσεξομολογησάμενοι): Lit., "to confess."
This term (προσεξομολογέω) is the only true
hapax legomenon in the *Didache*. Similar terms such
as προσομολογέω and ὁμολογέω appear in other
literature. Many editors prefer the emended form
προεξομολογέω (cf. Hilgenfeld 1884; Harnack
1884; Holmes 2007). *Break bread and give thanks:* Or,
"celebrate the Eucharist" if the phrase intends a
more formal liturgical experience.
14.2 *Dispute* (ἀμφιβολίαν): In classical Greek this

term means either "a state of mutual attack"
(Herodotus), "ambiguity" (Aristotle), or "doubt-
fulness" (Plutarch). It is not used in ApCon (Schaff
1885, 100).
15.1 *Bishops and deacons:* Lit., "overseers and ser-
vants" (ἐπισκόπους καὶ διακόνους).
15.2 *For they represent your integrity <in the same
way as do> the prophets and teachers:* Lit., "for they
are the honored among you together with the
prophets and teachers." This latter rendering is

15.3 Cf. ᵃTGad 6.3;
Mt 18:15
Cf. ᵇ1Cor 5:11
15.4 Cf. Mt 6:1–18
16.1 Cf. Mt 24:42, 44;
25:13; Mk 13:35, 37,
33; Lk 12:35, 40
16.3 Cf. ᵃMt 24:10–
12; Mk 13:13a
Cf. ᵇMt 7:15; Mk
13:22
16.4 Cf. ᵃ1Jn 2:18, 22;
4:3; 2Jn 7
Cf. ᵇMt 24:10
Cf. ᶜMt 24:24
Cf. ᵈJoel 2:2

teachers. ³And do not correct one another in anger but in peace, as you have in the gospel. And each one who sins against another, let no one speak <to them> nor let <them> hear from you until they repent (μετανοήσῃ). ⁴And offer your prayers and charity and all your actions just as you discern (ἔχετε) in the gospel of our Lord.

16 Watch over your life. Do not let [your] lamps go out and be caught unprepared, but be ready. For you do not know the hour in which our Lord comes. ²And meet together frequently, seeking what is beneficial for yourselves. For the whole time (χρόνος) of your faith will not benefit you if you are not complete at the last moment (καιρῷ). ³For false prophets and corruptors will be plentiful in the last days, and sheep will be changed into wolves, and love will be changed into hate. ⁴For with the spread of anarchy (ἀνομίας) they will hate and harass and betray one another. And then the

patrons, the reason for success" (ὑμεῖς δὲ τιμᾶτε τούτους ὡς πατέρας, ὡς κυρίους, ὡς εὐεργέτας, ὡς τοῦ εὖ εἶναι αἰτίους).
15.3 • Peace . . . until they repent: ApCon offers "mildness, with kindness and peace" (μακροθυμίᾳ μετὰ χρηστότητος καὶ εἰρήνης).†
15.4 • And offer your prayers . . . gospel of the Lord: ApCon omits this verse, offering "observe all things that are commanded you by the Lord" (πάντα τὰ προστεταγμένα ὑμῖν ὑπὸ τοῦ κυρίου φυλάξατε). As you discern: Lit., "as you have" (ὡς ἔχετε). Geor reads "as you perceive" (ἐμάθετε). Of our Lord: Geor adds "Jesus Christ" (Ἰησοῦ Χριστοῦ).
16.1 • Your life (ζωῆς ὑμῶν): Geor omits "your" (ὑμῶν). Do not let . . . in which our Lord comes: ApCon offers a different reading entirely.† [Your] lamps (αἱ ὀσφύες ὑμῶν): Emendation by Bryennios following ApCon (as with 14.1–2 above). H reads "our lamps" (αἱ ὀσφύες ἡμῶν).†
16.2 • And meet together . . . for yourselves: Omitted by ApCon. Will not benefit you (οὐ . . . ὠφελήσει ὑμᾶς): H and Barn agree on this reading. ApCon offers "will not profit you" (οὐ . . . ὀνήσει ὑμᾶς). The whole time of your faith . . . if you are not complete at the last moment: Geor adds "by faith and love" (τῇ πίστει καὶ ἀγάπῃ). ApCon reads "the things that have been done, if at the end of your life you stray from the true faith" (τὰ πρότερα κατορθώματα, ἐὰν εἰς τὰ ἔσχατα ὑμῶν ἀποπλανηθῆτε τῆς πίστεως τῆς ἀληθοῦς).
16.3 • Corruptors: ApCon adds "of the word" (τοῦ λόγου). Love will be changed into hate: ApCon omits "will be changed" (στραφήσεται).
16.4 • With the spread of (αὐξανούσης): ApCon reads "through the increase of" (πληθυνθείσης) following Matt 24:12. Anarchy: ApCon follows Matt 24:12 and adds "the love of many will grow cold" (ψυγήσεται ἡ ἀγάπη τῶν πολλῶν). They will hate . . . one another (μισήσουσιν ἀλλήλους): ApCon offers "for

more common among translators, but the text seems to hint that it is not the honor of the ministers themselves that matter but, instead, the honor of the community of faith that they represent.
16.1 *And be caught unprepared*: Lit., "and do not let your waists be unrobed" (καὶ αἱ ὀσφύες ὑμῶν

μὴ ἐκλυέσθωσαν). The clear reference is to being ready and appropriately dressed for action rather than relaxed and caught unaware.
16.2 *Yourselves*: Lit., "your souls/lives" (ψυχαῖς; cf. 2.7; 3.9).

deceiver of the world will appear as a son of God and perform signs and wonders, and the earth will be handed over into his hands, and he will do such atrocities as have never existed before. ⁵Then all humanity will come to the fire of testing, and many will fall away and perish. But those who persist in their faith will be saved by the cursed one himself. ⁶And then the signs of truth will appear: a first sign of an opening in the sky, then a sign of a trumpet sound, and the third—the raising of the dead. ⁷Yet not of all <the dead>, but as it has been said: "The Lord will come, and all the holy ones with him." ⁸Then the world will see the Lord coming on the clouds of the sky . . .

16.5 Cf. ᵃ1Cor 3:13; 1Pt 1:7
Cf. ᵇZech 13:8–9
Cf. ᶜMt 24:10
Cf. ᵈMt 10:22; 24:13; Mk 13:13b
16.6 Cf. Mt 24:30–31; 1Cor 15:52; 1Th 4:16
16.7 Cf. Zech 14:5; Mt 25:31; 1Th 3:13
16:8 Cf. Dan 7:13; Mt 16:27; 24:30; 26:64; Mk 13:26; Lk 21:27

men will hate one another" (μισήσουσιν γάρ ἀλλήλους οἱ ἄνθρωποι). Betray (παραδώσουσιν): ApCon uses the form προδώσουσιν. As a son of God . . .: ApCon offers an alternative reading.†
16.5 • Then all humanity . . . fire of testing: ApCon omits this clause. And perish (καὶ ἀπολοῦνται): ApCon reads "because of him" (ἐπ᾽ αὐτῷ). In their faith (ἐν τῇ πίστει αὐτῶν): ApCon follows Matt 24:13 and offers "to the end, they themselves" (εἰς τέλος, οὗτοι). By the cursed one himself (ὑπ᾽ αὐτοῦ τοῦ καταθέματος): Geor reads "because of . . ." (ἀπ᾽ αὐτοῦ . . .). ApCon omits this phrase.†
16.6 • The signs of truth . . . opening in the sky: ApCon follows Matt 24:30 and reads "the sign of the son of man in the sky" (τὸ σημεῖον τοῦ υἱοῦ τοῦ ἀνθρώπου ἐν τῷ οὐρανῷ). Dida uses the phrase "sign of extension" (signum . . . extensionis) in agreement with the phrase "sign of an opening" (σημεῖον ἐκπετάσεως) in H, though here the phrase is applied to the figure and teachings of Jesus specifically (Connolly 1923, 152–53).† A sign of a trumpet . . . raising of the dead: ApCon offers here "shall be a trumpet sound by an archangel and at the same time a raising of those who sleep" (φωνὴ σάλπιγγος ἔσται δι᾽ ἀρχαγγέλου καὶ μεταξὺ ἀναβίωσις τῶν κεκοιμημένων).
16.7 • Yet not of all <the dead>, but as it has been said: ApCon reads simply "and then" (καὶ τότε).† The holy ones: Geor adds "of him" (αὐτοῦ), thus to read "his holy ones."
16.8 • Then the world will see the Lord coming: ApCon offers "with quaking" (ἐν συσσεισμῷ). The world: Geor adds "itself" (οὗτος). Of the sky: ApCon follows Matt 16:27 and adds "with angels of his power on a throne of <his> kingdom" (μετ᾽ ἀγγέλων δυνάμεως αὐτοῦ ἐπὶ θρόνου βασιλείας). Geor follows Matt 24:30 and adds "with power and great glory" (μετὰ δυνάμεως καὶ δόξης πολλῆς).†

16.4 *Deceiver of the world* (κοσμοπλανής): Read κοσμοπλάνος (Harnack 1886; Knopf 1920). The term πλάνος is used in classical literature to indicate "wanderer," but in the NT to mean "deceiver." Rev 12:9 employs the word in the same way as the Didachist, but associates the figure more specifically with the devil or Satan.
16.5 *All humanity*: Lit., "the creation of humankind" (ή κτίσις τῶν ἀνθρώπων). *By the cursed one himself*: The meaning of this phrase is uncertain and may refer either to something cursed or to someone who has been cursed (as translated here).
16.6 *Opening* (ἐκπετάσεως): This term (ἐκπέτασις) is used in Plutarch (*De Sera Numinis Vindicta* 23) to mean "a spreading out," and the verbal form ἐκπετάννυμι is employed in Job 26:9: "[God] covers the full moon's face and *spreads out* his cloud over it." The logic is different in the *Didache*, however, since the author's purpose is to depict a significant spreading of the clouds so as to create a rift through which "the Lord" (either God or Christ) and accompanying figures may descend.

ADDITIONAL NOTES

1.1 *There are two ways*: The title provides no indication of the "two ways" motif, though it is widely known from antiquity. Cf. Deut 30:15; Jer 21:8; Prov 12:28; Sir 15:17; TLevi 19.1; TAsh 1.5–9; 2 Enoch 30.15; 1QSa 3.13–4.1; Matt 7:13–14; Gal 5:17–18; Barn 18–20; HermMan 6.1.1–2.10; Targum Pseudo-Jonathan on Deut 30:15; Strom 5.5 (van de Sandt and Flusser 2002, 140–90; Milavec 2003, 62–65). This appears to be the oldest part of the tradition, perhaps originally combined with the apocalyptic materials of chap. 16 (Drews 1904, 53–79). Its presence here suggests the text lies "in the mainstream of Judaism in setting this double commandment at the head" (Stewart 2011, 20). But the "two ways" circulated independently as a tradition before finding its home in the *Didache*. This is suggested especially by the extensive comparisons found with Barn, whose own approach is less exegetical in form and more typically that of an "ethical gnosis" (Kraft 1965, 134). Also, the transition from the "two ways" segment to instructions on praxis found at 6.2 is not shared by the closest parallel to the text, Doct, perhaps reinforcing the idea of autonomous transmission. Some scholars observe the possibility that the "two ways" tradition found later in Hermas was based to some extent on that preserved in the *Didache* (Giet 1970, 62).

One of life and one of death: Barnabas reads "one of light and one of darkness" (18.1). Hermas refers to two angels (versus "ways"), defined as "one of righteousness and one of wickedness" (HermMan 6.2.1). Pseudo-Clementines, in *Homilies* 5.7, offers "the flat and level way of the lost . . . and the narrow and rough way of the saved (ἡ τῶν ἀπολλυμένων ὁδὸς πλατεῖα καὶ ὁμαλωτάτη . . . ἡ δὲ τῶν σωζομένων στενὴ μὲν καὶ τραχεῖα). Doct follows a similar nomenclature in distinction from H. 1QSa identifies these as angels (//Hermas), but defines them by the characteristics of light and darkness (//Barn). The nature of "life and death" is defined in numerous contexts, often in association with baptismal rituals (Kamlah 1964; Suggs 1972).

1.2 *First, love God who made you; second, your neighbor as yourself*: Known independently from Hebrew scripture, these are combined in the gospels, which need not be the source of the teaching here; cf. TIss 5.1–2; TDan 5.3; Josephus, *Jewish War* 2.139; Philo, *On the Special Laws* 2.63 (Stewart 2011, 19–21). Scholars suggest this connection is the work of Jesus, though the independent witness of the *Didache* and separate use of the second commandment elsewhere recommends otherwise. The use of "lord God" in the Synoptics (following Deuteronomy) is not found here, though it is preserved in ApCon; conversely, *Didache*'s Jewish phrase "who made you" is not reflected in the Synoptics. The marks of redaction from the narrative tradition of the Synoptics are not evident.

Do not do to another: Here is the typical use of the negative form of the so-called "golden rule" (see Tob 4:15; Acts 15:20; *Aristides* 15.5; Irenaeus, *Against Heresies* 3.12.14; Strom 2.23), which conflicts with the rare positive usage in the Synoptics (also 1 Clem 13.1). The Synoptics are thus not likely the source of the *Didache* tradition. The connection between this rule and the previous double commandment to love may already be suggested in Matthew, however, which separates them in context but insists on the observation that each fulfills "the law and prophets" (so Matt 7:12; 22:40).

1.3–2.1 *Bless those who curse you . . . and a second instruction of the teaching <is this>*: This entire section is missing in CO, Doct, Epit, and Arab, suggesting its secondary insertion into H by a subsequent interpolator (Layton 1968, 343–83; Rordorf 1981, 499–513; Niederwimmer 1998, 22, 68–72). The passage is full of teachings of Jesus drawn from the Synoptic tradition, especially the Q source (Glover 1958, 12–29). Use of similar source materials finds no parallel elsewhere in

49

the text of the *Didache*, and thus it is undoubtedly appropriate to think of this section along the lines of a "Christian interpolation" (*interpolation christiana* or *sectio evangelica*). This runs counter to earlier scholarly views that, based upon the inclusion of these materials in Dida, ApCon, and H, argued for its original position within the *Vorlage* of the text (Connolly 1923, 156–57).

1.3 *Listen to what is necessary for you to do to save your spirit: first of all*: This insertion in POxy is missing in H and elsewhere. It probably reflects a similar idea from 1 Cor 5:5 ("that his spirit may be saved"). Since Pauline materials are not otherwise widely reflected in H, this parallel may suggest yet another secondary addition to the textual tradition, though admittedly quite early in the history of development.

Pray for your enemies: This instruction is not preserved specifically in the NT gospels, but is found elsewhere in the literary tradition as a teaching of Jesus. Cf. POxy 1224 and JusDia 133.6b (Kraft 1965, 139).

Fast for your persecutors: While this phrase may simply reflect Matt 5:44 (perhaps in oral form, since Matthew's "pray for" [προσεύχομαι] is now replaced by "fast for" [νηστεύω] in the *Didache*), subsequent intepretations of the teaching may suggest a later concern against the doctrinal errors of the Ebionites. Thus a parallel reading appears in Origen, *Homiliae in Leviticum* 10 (*invenimus in quodam libello ab apostolis dictum, "beatus est qui etiam jejunat pro eo ut alat pauperem"*). Epiphanius likewise quotes from ApCon in *Adversus haereses* 70.11 specifically about the Jews: "When [the Jews] feast, you shall fast and mourn for them" (Schaff 1885, 164).

1.4 *Reject the appeals of the flesh and body. If someone strikes you . . . also your tunic*: Though this passage opens with words that clearly belong to the Didachist (or more likely some later editor), the comments about striking, going the extra mile, and giving one's coat clearly reflect the teachings of Synoptic tradition (Rordorf 1981, 502; Schöllgen 1991, 100).

1.5 *Fortunate is the one who gives*: This is likely a reflection of Acts 20:35 ("It is more blessed to give than to receive"), as is suggested by the phrase of authority that follows, "according to <this> instruction" (κατὰ τὴν ἐντολήν). The indication of "instruction" or "commandment" designates a probable dominical saying in the mind of the author at this point. This is reinforced by the parallel in HermMan 2.4 ("Give to all, for God wishes that from his own gifts, gifts should be given to all"), which is further evidence that this well-known teaching on generosity circulated widely within the early church setting. At this same time, this instruction falls within what is probably a later addition to the text (1.3b–2.1), and thus perhaps comes from a secondary setting.

1.6 *Let your gift sweat in your hands*: This is one of the most provocative and enigmatic statements within the *Didache*. An approximate parallel exists in Sibylline Oracles 2.95—"Give to the needy with perspiring hand" (Mendelssohn 1890, 240–70)—though most editors consider the root of the teaching to derive from Sir 12:1. Later abuse of charity by idle panhandlers eventually led to the practice of dispensation through the office of the bishop, thus providing some oversight to the custom of almsgiving within the community. If this is actually the situation in which the teaching is offered here, it further suggests that 1.3b–2.1 is secondary to the text and somewhat later to the tradition of the *Vorlage*, reflecting a consciousness of ecclesiastical development in theology and praxis. The teaching itself, however, is undeniably old (Audet 1958, 275–80).

2.2–3.6 This section of the text is structured around the initial prohibitions of the Decalogue (Exod 20:7–17; Deut 5:7–21): murder, adultery, theft, covetousness, and false testimony. While these "great sins" are listed together with other elements in 2.2–7, the text interweaves them with a series of "lesser sins" in 3.1–6—in the style of a rabbinic *fence*—to prevent the listener from committing the more grievous transgressions (Taylor 1886, 23; Harris 1887, 80). This feature of the *Didache* is unique among parallel writings that feature the "two ways." It is unclear whether the structure should be attributed to the Didachist or to the source from which the prohibitions have been drawn (Audet 1958, 280–308).

2.5 *But you must act accordingly*: This difficult phrase takes a "tone of exception" not reflected in all texts of the tradition and perhaps suggesting its secondary insertion into H. Other phrases in the *Didache* have a similar function, as with "and you shall be satisfied" and "for you must not" (1.4), and "if you cannot, do what you can" (6.2). It is difficult to know whether this is the voice of the Didachist, but its presence in the "Christian interpolation" suggests the hand of a later editor who emended the text beyond the interpolation itself.

2.6 *You must not be a coveter . . . nor arrogant*. This list of warnings against evil actions has the look of ancient virtue-vice lists from antiquity (cf. 1 Cor 5:10). There is some reason to think that the Didachist has drawn upon similar teachings in the construction of this material, since they circulated widely among Christians, Jews, and Greeks (McDonald 1980).

2.7 *But reprimand some, pray for some*: This section is set apart in translation based on its absence in Doct. It is entirely possible that these words were not original to the tradition, having been inserted under the influence of Matt 18:15: "go, reprimand him" (ὕπαγε ἔλεγξον αὐτὸν). But one must consider that, taken together with 2.6b ("You must not conceive an evil plan against your neighbor"), these materials form a classic ABA′ pattern (Audet 1958, 294–95). The variant reading of CO may likewise indicate knowledge of Jude 22—"and be merciful to some who waver" (καὶ οὓς μὲν ἐλεᾶτε διακρινομένους)—though this does not speak to the issue of "pray for some" in the primary tradition. Presumably CO has substituted the "merciful" phrase for that of "prayer."

3.1–6 There is a structural cohesion to these verses that suggests a literary background. The source behind these materials remains unclear, though its foundation is likely derived from Jewish noncanonical tradition. Cf. TJud 14.1 (Kraft 1965, 146).

3.1 *My child*: This formal address appears in regular fashion several times in 3.1–4.1, though not as consistently in the parallel texts of Doct, ApCon, CO, and Epit. This may be due to stylistic differences among authors, including the tendency of CO to omit "my" (μου) throughout. Though used only in these verses, this element of sapiential literature is widely known among both Jewish and late Greek writings (Audet 1958, 302–5). It remains unclear why the Didachist has restricted its usage to this segment of the text, except to highlight the specific ways in which the Decalogue must be protected through wisdom teaching. It may be noteworthy that no similar form appears in the parallels of Barn, suggesting perhaps that the presence of this introductory phrase is unique to the "two ways" tradition of the *Didache* (Niederwimmer 1998, 94–102).

3.3 *Nor one who lifts up their eyes*: The term ὑψηλόφθαλμος first appears here in Greek literature (Schöllgen 1991, 107). The translation "lift up the eyes" is a literal rendering based on the root ὑψηλο–, indicating something that is "high" or "carried high," and ὀφθαλμός, meaning "eye," and is preferred by many interpreters of the text (Goodspeed 1950, 12; Milavec 2003, 19). Many other commentaries choose something more like "bold gazes" (Cody 1995, 6; followed by Niederwimmer 1998, 94; van de Sandt and Flusser 2002, 11), "eager gazer" (Schaff 1885, 172), or "roving eyes" (Kraft 1965, 147). This is suggested already by ApCon, which employs the term ῥιψόφθαλμος, meaning "to cast the eyes about," another word of rare usage in the literature (see Ptolemaeus, *Tetrabiblios* 164, 171). Either rendering is perhaps suitable, but the salacious action of dipping the chin and gazing upwards toward another person undoubtedly anticipates a more specific motivation than is suggested by the general enthusiasm of careless or lascivious gazing about.

3.4 *Nor wish to see them*: One is tempted to read with the tradition of Doct, CO, and Geor here: "nor wish to see or hear them" (Wengst 1984, 70). The textual tradition is obviously confused at this point, and the rhythm of the phrase "see or hear" reads well. This is likely the very rationale to reject such a balanced reading, however, based on the supposition of *lectio difficilior potior*.

3.7 *But be modest . . . the earth*: It is curious that, where H (followed by ApCon) reflects scriptural norms (Psalms and Matthew), other traditions alter the reading to a more exalted status: "holy ground" (Doct); "kingdom of heaven" (CO); "kingdom of God" (Epit). This clearly suggests a development in the tradition that works away from biblical foundations, but has not yet settled on a single concept. One might argue that CO and Epit suggest some dependence on the tradition behind Doct, if not necessarily on Doct itself.

At the same time, Dida probably is dependent on the *Didache* (or less likely Barn 19.4) here, employing Isa 66:2 with Matt 5:5 in this process as a means by which to instruct bishops (Connolly 1923, 150–51). The text reads at 2.1.5:

> Thus, though he is young, nothwithstanding how humble, fainthearted, and quiet he may be, as the Lord said through Isaiah: To whom shall I look if not the humble and quiet who tremble at my word? It likewise says in the gospel: Blessed are the modest, who shall inherit the earth.

> *Unde etiamsi iuvenis est, tamen ut mansuetus sit, timidus et quietus, quoniam dicit per Eseiam dominus Deus—Super quem respiciam nisi super mansuetum et quietum et trementem verba mea semper? Similiter et in evangelio dicit ita—Beati mansueti, quia ipsi hereditabunt terram.*

3.10 *Receive the things that happen to you as good*: This teaching is widely found in one form or another among Stoic, Jewish, biblical, and Christian traditions (Niederwimmer 1998, 102). Within Christian circles one need look no further than the vague scriptural parallels at Matt 10:29//Luke 12:6, Acts 27:34b, and Rom 8:28. These are encapsulated in later teachings, as appear for example in Origen, *De principiis* 3.2.7 and Dorotheus, *Epistulae* 3 (1040C).

4.1–8 This segment stands as a subset within the larger "two ways" section, advocating rules for the common life of the community (Schöllgen 1991, 109). The perspective is that of a teacher who is inspired by the perspective of the Word of God, perhaps suggesting a designation within a larger office of teaching (Neymeyr 1989, 139–40).

4.1 *Of <the> Lord*: The present translation is an intentional circumlocution of the term κυριότης, leaving the concept undefined. Generally translated as "power, lordship, dominion" (HermSim 5.6.1; Jude 8; 2 Pet 2:10; Thom 90) or some sort of spiritual or angelic power (2 Enoch 61.10; Eph 1:21; Col 1:16) elsewhere in literature, the word is imprecise, resulting in varied proposals here, such as "lordship" (Kleist 1948, 17; [*souveraineté*] Refoulé 1990, 49; Cody 1995, 7; [*souveraineté*] Rordorf and Tuilier 1998, 159; Ehrman 2003, 1:423), "Lord's nature" (Goodspeed 1950, 13; [*Wesen*] Lindemann and Paulsen 1992, 9; Holmes 2007, 351), "doctrine of the Lord" (Glimm 1947, 174), "dominion" (Milavec 2003, 21), and "kingship" (Kraft 1978, 311).

There <the> Lord is: Apart from parallels to Matthew, similar use of the phrase in *Pirqe Abot* 3.3 refers to the presence of the Shekinah among those who study Torah based on an interpretation of Mal 3:16. This reflects a long tradition of interpretation found elsewhere in Jewish literature (Taylor 1969, 43–44 n. 8). This concept was favored in the later Arabic *Life of Shenoute* as a reflection of ancient tradition about the significance of fidelity to ministers. To that end, it undoubtedly reflects a primitive concept typical of "two ways" teaching (Iselin 1895, 20; Giet 1970, 134).

This phrase is difficult to translate without insertion of the definite article, but no manuscript includes the article. This is even true for CO, which includes an article in the phrase "as the Lord" (ὡς τὸν κύριον) found earlier in the verse, but does not do so here.

The phrase "as Lord" (ὡς κύριον) appears here and at 11.2 and 4 in H. It is assumed in each case that the author wishes to indicate some "lordly" characteristic of the person involved rather than to make a comparison of that individual with "the Lord," as most translators suppose.

4.2 *So that you may find comfort in their words*: These words likely suggest provisions for correction within the community. The practice of communal support has a long tradition in Judaism and patristic Christianity beginning already with 1QS 6.6–8. Cf. AposTrad 35.2; 41.2–3; *Rule of Pachomius* 115 (Rordorf and Tuilier 1998, 158–59 n. 4).

4.6 *Make some reparation for your sins:* Though the *Didache* does not make use of Tobit, this is an estimable reflection of the tradition of Tob 4:8–10 and the concept of storing up credit with God. Cf. HermMan 2.4.

4.8 *For the Lord wants for all to be given from his gifts:* This line appears here in Doct (*omnibus enim dominus dare vult de donis suis sententiam*) but in 1.5 of H (πᾶσι γὰρ θέλει δίδασθαι ὁ πατὴρ ἐκ τῶν ἰδίων χαρισμάτων). This raises a textual problem, since Doct does not include the materials of 1.3b–2.1 as found in H, which are thus generally considered by scholars to be secondary to the text (POxy is not helpful here, since it does not continue into vs. 5). One solution would be to imagine that this line originally stood here in H as well, presumably having then been transposed into the materials of 1.3b–2.1 when the remaining materials of that segment was added by a later editor (Wengst 1984, 72). Another solution would be that the author of Doct saved 1.5 to this position when the wording of 1.3b–2.1 was removed. This second solution seems less likely, however, since there is no clear reason why the segment would have been removed from the text.

4.9–11 This section contains a limited version of the so-called "household codes" of community life that circulated in various forms throughout ancient Greek, Jewish, and Christian literature. Cf. Seneca, *Epistulae moralis* 91.1–3; Cicero, *De officiis* 1.3; Epictetus, *Dissertationes* 2.17, 31; Dio Chrysostom, *De regno* 4.91; Sir 7:18–35; Philo, *On the Decalogue* 165–67; Josephus, *Jewish Antiquities* 2.190–209; Col 3:18–4:1; Eph 5:21–6:9; 1 Pet 2:11–3:12; 1 Clem 1.3; 21.6–9. Such rules were widely employed within the church until that time when (in the mid-second century?) the authority of bishops was firmly established, and subsequently this literary form of instruction became a hindrance (Jefford 1997, 121–27).

4.13 ApCon inserts *from him . . . to them . . . from them* throughout as logical completions of grammatical structure within the verse that might be expected by the listener. While the presence of such words argues against their authenticity with relation to the *Vorlage*, their absence in H attests to the rustic character of the Didachist's use of Greek and grammatical phrases.

4.14 *In the community:* This phrase finds no parallel elsewhere in the textual witnesses. In fact, the entirety of the opening instruction about disclosure of wrongdoings is missing in Doct. It seems obvious that the phrase is secondary to the tradition, probably added by a later hand in the light of the verbal parallel found at Jas 5:16. It is translated here as an expected element from the exemplar, but is not likely authentic to the *Vorlage*.

5.1–2 *But the way of death is this:* This is the last section of the "two ways" sequence, but it is by far the shortest. The secondary prohibitions that were constructed to protect the Decalogue (chaps. 2–3) and the introductory use of the phrase "my child" (chaps. 3–4), so typical of wisdom literature, are no longer present here. The focus thus is primarily on elements of the Decalogue.

A comparison of vice lists as found in Barn (20.1c) and H (5.1c–d) raises numerous problems. The *Didache* version is longer, containing all items in the Barn list except for the term "transgression" (παράβασις). The sequence in Barn also begins with "idolatry" (εἰδωλολατρία), a concern of Barn elsewhere (4.8; 9.6; 16.7), but not so much in the *Didache*. Structurally, it seems that the Didachist's listing of elements has been "reorganized and expanded significantly" with the evolution of its tradition, suggested largely by a comparison of elements with ancient parallels (cf. Wis 14:12–31; TLevi 17:11; 2 Enoch 34:1), and other early Christian writings (cf. Rom 1:23; 1 Clem 35.3; HermMan 6.2.5; JusDia 95.1; Theophilus, *To Autolycus* 2.34–35). In comparison with Doct, the prominent elements in the list are "adulteries, murders, false testimonies" (*moechationes, homicidia, falsa testimonia*), which again are not in agreement with H (Kraft 1965, 156–59).

6.1–3 These verses clearly represent the ending of the "two ways" materials in the *Didache*. This is particularly evident in Doct, for which this is the conclusion of the entire work. Though Doct reads similarly to H in concept, the reference to the "whole yoke of the Lord" and the exception clause of "do what you can" in H (6.2), as well as the warning against food sacrificed to idols (6.3), are not found in the Latin. Doct also concludes differently with the mention of "the Lord Jesus Christ" not otherwise found in the christology of H (*per dominum Iesum Christum regnantem et dominantem cum deo patre et spiritu sancto in saecula saeculorum. amen*).

Barn is even more diverse in comparison with both H and Doct, though the author of that text also recognizes that some conclusion is appropriate here. Barn consequently reads:

Thus it is good to learn the righteous ways of the Lord written here in order to walk in them. For the one who does these things will receive glory in the kingdom of God; the one who chooses otherwise will perish along with their works. This is why there is a resurrection; this is why there is reparation.

καλὸν οὖν ἐστίν, μαθόντα τὰ δικαιώματα τοῦ κυρίου ὅσα γέγραπται, ἐν τούτοις περιπατεῖν. ὁ γὰρ ταῦτα ποιῶν ἐν τῇ βασιλείᾳ τοῦ θεοῦ δοξασθήσεται· ὁ ἐκεῖνα ἐκλεγόμενος μετὰ τῶν ἔργων αὐτοῦ συναπολεῖται. διὰ τοῦτο ἀνάστασις, διὰ τοῦτο ἀνταπόδομα.

There is clearly a return to the "two ways" motif found at the beginning of the section (Barn 18.1–2; cf. Did 1.1), which includes an eschatological element not otherwise found in H or Doct. There may be some reason to think that a similar focus was originally associated with the "two ways" of the *Didache* if chapter 16 once served as the conclusion to these materials before the insertion of chapters 7–15.

Also interesting is the material that appears here in ApCon, which retains only minimal aspects of the tradition known from H: "see that no one diverts you from . . ."; "and regarding foods"; and "shun idols, for they sacrifice to them in honor of demons." Typical of the author, scripture from Neh 8:10 is incorporated here, and 1 Cor 10:20 ("what they sacrifice is to demons and not to God") has clearly been used to shape the closing comment about sacrificing to idols. But beyond this deviation from H, the author has maintained the περί δέ ("and regarding") formula to introduce the topic of foods that may be eaten. This is highly significant, since the formula continues both in H and ApCon as an introduction to teachings on baptism (7.1), eucharistic prayers (9.1, 3; 10.1 [=μετά δέ]), and prophets and apostles (11.3). The author of ApCon thus appears to understand the unity of these materials as a collected unit of teachings despite feeling the freedom to adapt the materials in 6.1–3 into a form that diverges from the comments found in H.

Finally, ApCon agrees with Doct in its omission of references to the "whole yoke of the Lord" or the exception clause of "do what you can" (6.2). This seems further reason to think that these materials may not be original to the *Vorlage* behind H, but may instead represent the editorial work of a later hand (Audet 1958, 352–57).

6.3–11.12 The Didachist turns here to a new section identified by a series of teachings on appropriate foods, baptism, fasting, prayer, and itinerant apostles and prophets that are identified by the use of the περὶ δέ formula in H (see 6.3; 7.1; 9.1, 3; 10.1 [=μετὰ δὲ]; 11.3). These materials serve as a transition between the "two ways" teachings of 1.1–6.2 and the instructions on how to welcome outsiders into the community, community regulations, and a final warning found in 12.1–16.8. At the same time, the core teachings found here suggest that these materials are intended to function in a regulatory capacity for the daily lifestyle of community members.

7.1–4 These verses on baptism find no parallel within the tradition except in ApCon, and here only in a much developed form. The text of H is concerned to maintain the traditional trappings of Jewish proselyte baptism with its focus on "running water" in sympathy with the instructions for cleansing found in Lev 15:13. The restriction that the water be "cold" suggests that it should be fresh, not gathered from a cistern and permitted to sit for a time, suggesting the typical nature of Jewish *mikva'ot* that were used for rituals of purification.

Three elements within this material suggest later additions, however: the incorporation of the Trinitarian formula (7.1) and the instruction to "pour water on the head three times" in sympathy with that image (7.3); permission to use water that is not "running" or "cold" if necessary (7.2); and, an insistence that both the baptizer and the one to be baptized fast prior to the event (7.4). Such concerns for theology and ritual might be considered more typical of later ecclesiastical practice than one might expect for a text as early as the *Didache* (Schaff 1885, 41–57; Audet 1958, 357–67; McDonald 1980, 188 n. 174).

But despite the expectation that such elements might be found suitable for ecclesiastical ritual, the ApCon includes none of them in its own reading here. Thus, one reads:

Now regarding baptism, oh bishop or presbyter, we gave direction and now say that you shall baptize as the Lord commanded us, saying, "Go, teach all nations, baptizing them in the name of the Father, Son, and Holy Spirit, teaching them to observe all I commanded you," of the Father who sent, Christ who came, and Comforter who witnessed. But first anoint the person with holy oil and then baptize with water, and lastly seal with ointment that the anointing with oil may be sharing in the Holy Spirit, the water a symbol of Christ's death, and the ointment a seal of covenants. But if no oil or ointment is available, water is ample for the anointing, seal, and confession of the one who is dead or dying with Christ. But before baptism, let the one to be baptized fast, for even the Lord when first baptized by John and remaining in the wilderness did then fast forty days and nights. He was baptized and then fasted, not needing cleansing, fasting, or purging, being naturally pure and holy, but so he might witness the truth to John and give us an example.

Our Lord was thus not baptized into his own passion, death, or resurrection (for none of these then happened) but for another reason. He fasted by his own authority after baptism, being John's Lord. So the one to be initiated into that death should first fast and then be baptized. For it is unreasonable that one who is buried with Christ and risen with him should be dejected at his resurrection. For a person is not lord of our Savior's being, since one is master and the other servant.

The materials in ApCon clearly speak to biblical considerations (so Matt 28:19), the need to explain the link between Christian baptism and that of Jesus of Nazareth (cf. IgnEph 18.2), and an urgency to avoid any assumption that Christ was himself saved through his own baptism. These are theological concerns that reflect long years of speculation. The elements that H features (Trinitarian language; exceptions about the water; role of both the baptizer and catechumen) would fit nicely into such a structure, but are in fact absent in ApCon, except of course where ApCon quotes directly from Matt 28:19.

It seems less likely then that ApCon chose to omit these elements from the *Vorlage*, presumably represented by a tradition similar to that of H, than that they never existed in the manuscript that the author received. If this is indeed true, then what now appears in *Didache* 7 is most likely secondary to its original form, which was primarily concerned with the instruction on fasting in association with baptizing.

8.1–3 The instruction on prayer offers concerns that reflect typical Jewish practices. Thus the reference to "second and fifth <days> after the sabbath" versus "fourth <day> and day of preparation" are focused specifically on prayer associated with synagogue worship. Eth supersedes the instruction here by insisting that prayer be conducted all "five days."

The reference to "hypocrites" remains unclear as to whether the author intends Jews who practice falsely (as with Matt 6:2, 5, 16), non-Jewish proselytes who attempt to justify their inclusion into the synagogue, or a specific constituent of Jews who practice their prayer in conflict with the organization of the *Didache*. Dida reflects a much more dominical awareness of the passage (5.14.18–21), forbidding readers to fast "in the custom of the former people, but according to the new covenant" that Jesus taught. Further, fasting is not to be for the sake of Christ but for the Jews themselves (Connolly 1923, 151–52).

As the Lord instructed in his gospel: This is the first use of the term "gospel" (εὐαγγέλιον) in the text, a word that has engendered significant discussion about whether this means "gospel tradition," perhaps oral in nature, or knowledge of a "written gospel," such as Matthew. The formulation of H ("in his gospel") may suggest the former, while the reading of ApCon and Eth ("in the gospel") doubtless assumes the latter. In either case, the phrase is unnecessary to the underlying instruction of 8.2 ("And do not pray like the hypocrites but . . . pray as follows") and may be secondary.

The so-called Lord's prayer that follows is remarkably close to the form preserved in Matt 6:9b–13, including the doxological elements that typify later manuscript traditions. This may be explained by the highly liturgical structure of the prayer (versus its parallel in Luke 11:2–4) that was widely known by early Christians and is generally employed today, or it may represent a link to the Matthean community tradition. Otherwise, it is once again possible that the prayer has been inserted at this juncture secondarily. The version in ApCon shows more conformity to the Matthean formula with use of phrases such as "in the heavens" and "our debts," in addition to the more complete reading of "for yours are the kingdom and the power" and the concluding "amen." It is also possible that ApCon simply reflects the more commonly used form of the prayer known to the author rather than following the text of H in a strict fashion.

9.2 *For the holy vine your child David . . . your child Jesus—yours . . .*: The only parallel to this prayer in the literature appears with significant alteration in ApCon (7.25.1–4). It is entirely possible that this alteration represents two separate hands or at least a secondary insertion that has changed the original reading (thus Wengst 1984, 78: *habent hanc sententiam secundo loco, sententiam de pane primo loco*). This suggestion is made in light of the confessional nature of the probable insertion, indicated here by italics:

for that life you made known to us by Jesus your Son, *through whom you made all things and take care of the world, whom you sent to be as human for our salvation, whom you let suffer and die, whom you raised and were pleased to glorify and set on your right hand, by whom you promised us resurrection from the dead . . .* for through him glory is also given forever. Amen.

The ellipsis in this passage represents a theme that is generally reflected in Did 9.4 ("this broken bread was scattered over the hills"), though ApCon has combined it with elements "concerning the precious blood of Jesus Christ" (ὑπὲρ τοῦ τιμίου αἵματος Ἰησοῦ Χριστοῦ) and "his precious blood" (τοῦ τιμίου σώματος), which likely reflects the influence of 1 Cor 11:26 and is not otherwise seen in the theology of the *Didache*.

9.4 *For yours are the power and the glory through Jesus Christ forever*: This is the only place in the *Didache* where the term "Christ" (Χριστός) is used. Since it appears here within a formulaic expression, one might have expected to see it already in the immediately preceding verse (9.3) where the text reads simply "yours is the glory forever." The entire phrase is missing in ApCon, which is especially curious, since the author of that text is noticeably more careful to include heightened theological terminology. One thus suspects that the phrase "through Jesus Christ" (διὰ Ἰησοῦ Χριστοῦ) was not originally found in the *Vorlage* (Peterson 1959, 146–82) and thus should be omitted from contemporary reconstructions of the text. Admittedly, related cognates appear in later chapters, terms such as "Christian" (Χριστιανός) in 12.4 and "Christ peddler" (χριστέμπορος) in 12.5, but the former is commonly known in literature and the latter appears first only here in the *Didache*. Like the phrase "through Jesus Christ," both of these may be later additions as well.

9.5 *Do not give what is holy to dogs*: This well-known phrase appears in the *Didache* as a likely reflection of the saying in Matt 7:6a, though the context is different for each. Because it is not preserved in ApCon, it also is likely a secondary intrusion into the *Vorlage* by a later hand, as with "through Jesus Christ" in 9.4. But there is otherwise no reason to think that it may not be original to the text.

10.7 *But allow the prophets to give thanks as they wish*: The shift from this phrase in H to that of ApCon ("but also permit your prophets to give thanks") indicates a subtle transition of office within the early church context. The Didachist offers no distinction between the function of prophet and the role of leadership within the community, regardless of whatever distinction may have been in the author's mind (Jefford 2010, 297–303, 313). ApCon, on the other hand, transfers the issue from one of *function* ("prophets") to one of *office* ("presbyters"), thus to suggest that the concern is more about the definition of status with respect to a particular agent within the ecclesiastical setting than it is about how spirit-filled persons (perhaps outsiders?) may celebrate a liturgical event. While such a concern may indeed have been in the mind of the Didachist, the shift from prophet to presbyter by ApCon removes any opportunity for individual expression within the ritual, undoubtedly by the design of the author.

10.8 Both Copt and ApCon add a verse here related to a prayer over the "ointment" (in Copt, ⲥⲧⲓⲛⲟⲩϥⲓ; in ApCon, μύρον) that is not found in H. While some scholars accept this tradition as authentic to the *Vorlage* behind H (Wengst 1984, 82), this is not entirely clear and is difficult to determine from the limited evidence that is available. As Niederwimmer reconstructs the text, the passage was not originally present in the *Didache*. The "ointment" prayer was likely interpolated either around the year 200 CE or slightly earlier, was then incorporated into ApCon with alterations, and the "noninterpolated" text continued in the forms now known from the witnesses of H and Geor (Niederwimmer 1989, 167). Copt then would be a witness to this interpolation, but without the alterations provided by ApCon.

11.2 *But if the one who teaches . . . do not listen to them*: Apart from the divergent readings of H (and Copt) and ApCon here, the two texts offer different justifications for the instruction. H continues with an exception clause to the effect that one who provides "righteousness and knowledge of the Lord" (δικαιοσύνην καὶ γνῶσιν κυρίου) should be accepted "as Lord" (ὡς κύριον), while apostles and prophets (so 11.3) should similarly be received as indicated in the "decree of the gospel" (κατὰ τὸ δόγμα τοῦ εὐαγγελίου). ApCon reads simply "for this one offends rather than glorifies God" (ὑβρίζει γὰρ ὁ τοιοῦτος τὸν θεὸν ἥπερ δοξάζει).

If the author of ApCon had these materials from Did 11.2b–3 available for inclusion, there is no obvious reason why they should be omitted in favor of the shorter comment that now stands in their place. It seems more logical that the *Vorlage* behind ApCon did not include such words (though attested generally by both the Greek and Coptic manuscripts) and that the tradition behind H and Copt was itself subsequently altered to include them. This idea may be reinforced by the suggestion that the author of these materials could have the apostle Paul's associate Timothy in mind as indicated by 1 Cor 4:17, though such parallels are not otherwise typical of the *Didache* (Audet 1958, 434).

The exception clause of 11.2b clearly reflects similar concessions at 6.2 and 7.2–3, which may themselves be secondary to the tradition. Otherwise, while the phrase "as Lord" appears in 4.1 and 11.4 of H, it too is omitted by ApCon at both places and likewise should not be considered original to the text (Wengst 1984, 82). Nor is "decree" (δόγμα) used here in ApCon. In conclusion, if the suggestion may be accepted that these materials are secondary to the *Didache* tradition, then the reference to "the gospel" in 11.3 should be understood only as knowledge of a written gospel text by a later editor rather than as evidence of some ancient gospel tradition known by the Didachist.

11.6 *Ask for money*: The Greek text of H advises that an apostle should not seek support from a host beyond the simple provisions of necessity, such as sustenance and lodging. To request otherwise would be a sign of false intention unworthy of a true apostle. Eth suggests more than this, using instead a word that may mean either "receive" or "take," and by extension in its nominal form, "theft." This shifts the concerns of the Didachist into a clearer situation, since thieves, who cannot be considered holy persons, by extension can hardly be counted as worthy of the definition "apostle."

11.7 *For every sin will be forgiven, but this sin will not be forgiven*: This comment clearly reflects the teaching of Matt 12:31, which alone uses the term "sin" (ἁμαρτία) over against its parallels in Mark 3:28–30 and Luke 12:10. The omission of this observation from the text of Eth is remarkable, however, since there is no obvious reason why such a justification for testing the spirit of an apostle (already recognized by Geor as the "holy spirit") should be passed over, especially since Eth thereafter resumes with the text at 11.8. While it is certainly possible that the source text behind Eth did not contain the phrase, it is once more likely that this comment in H has been added secondarily in the light of the Matthean reading.

11.8 *The Lord's traits*: This phrase (lit., "the ways of the Lord") carries a meaning that is not entirely clear. The word τρόπος, translated here as "traits," carries a variety of similar meanings, including "manner, way, guise, way of life, conduct, character, or frame of mind," sometimes used of persons and animals, other times of God (cf. 2 Macc 5:27; Acts 1:11; Rom 3:2). One might be tempted to offer the translation "way of life" as a reflection of the teaching of Did 1.1, but this is not demanded by the current context of the reference. Copt offers the translation "ways of the Lord" (ⲉⲛⲉⲥⲙⲁⲧ ⲙ̄ⲡⲭ̄ⲥ̄) as an apt understanding, though this does nothing to clarify the meaning of the author's intention. Eth alters the wording to the phrase "traits of God" for "Lord's traits" as rendered by H, thus indicating that the intended reference should be some attribute of divinity rather than that the reader should compare the prophet "who speaks in a spirit" with the figure of Jesus. Yet this view may be unique to the interpretative tradition of Eth and does not necessarily satisfy the question of the original author's purpose.

11.9 *In a spirit*: The motivation behind the actions of the presumed prophet is viewed differently between H and Copt here. The author of H, followed by Eth, fears that a prophet may choose to request and consume food by a claim of spiritual prerogative that is unwarranted, while Copt anticipates the problem of someone who arranges an occasion of ritual importance within the community yet stands aloof from the event. The former concern is motivated by individual desire, while the latter suggests the assumption of spiritual superiority that cannot be tolerated if the cohesion of the community and its rituals are to be maintained.

11.11 *A worldly mystery*: This phrase (εἰς μυστήριον κοσμικὸν) is particularly difficult to "understand, translate, and interpret" (Palmer 2011, 9 n. 65) from the perspective of the Didachist, and many translators provide a mystical sense to its understanding. But to offer such a meaning does not acknowledge the negative sense in which the phrase is presented, since the author then provides the caveat "even if not teaching <others> to act the same." Copt preserves the negative sense of the phrase with the words "worldly tradition" (ⲡⲁⲣⲁⲇⲱⲥⲓⲥ ⲛ̄ⲕⲱⲥⲙⲉⲓⲕⲱⲛ), though providing the Greek παράδοσις in place of the awkward μυστήριον, which is otherwise not commonly found in Greek literature. There may thus be some reason to think that the wording of H is secondary, with the terminology of Copt a better reflection of the original teaching. Eth provides an interesting confirmation of the negative tenor of the text, though clearly understanding "assembly" (ἐκκλησία) in a more ecclesiastical sense (and thus for Eth perhaps better rendered "church") with its disdain for those who act inappropriately within that holy setting.

12.1 *For you [will] have understanding*: This is a difficult phrase in the textual tradition, as is indicated by the confusion among the manuscript readings. Bryennios already has altered H to a future form that suggests the reader will obtain understanding when the occasion demands such. This is the reading that is accepted in the translation here. Eth indicates instead that the reader, presumably by the very nature of their confession, already possesses sufficient knowledge to make correct decisions. This is reinforced by the specific nature of the Copt, which insists that "you yourselves know" versus others who do not, and likewise by ApCon in its more complex use of "to have" (ἔχω) and "to be able" (δύναμαι) to know. It is quite possible that this latter view, represented by Copt and ApCon, actually reflects the intention of the Didachist. If so, then more emphasis should be placed on the mystical nature of the believer's confession than is otherwise assumed by the present translation.

13.3–7 *So taking all the first yield . . . give according to the instruction.* The Didachist applies the precepts of Numbers 18 to the situation of Christian prophets with the comment that "they are your high priests." This is viewed in sympathy with parallel teachings found within the NT (cf. Draper 2005). When no prophet is present, then the poor are to receive these elements. Conversely, ApCon makes no mention of prophets but more closely follows the intention of scripture by speaking of gifts made directly to priests (a logical rendering in this case, since the text is designed for instruction of Christian priests). A tenth of everything is to be given to orphans, widows, the poor, and strangers. The text for this chapter is problematic, since Eth often follows the reading of H but sometimes is in agreement with ApCon. This ambivalence on the part of Eth suggests the tradition behind the teaching here was not stable, thus making it difficult to determine the more likely form of the *Vorlage* based on a comparison of H and ApCon. While some scholars believe this entire segment to be the work of an interpolator (Audet 1958, 457–58), it is more likely that some original framework existed in the *Vorlage* behind H whose specific parameters have now been lost.

Dida understands the tradition similarly to ApCon, though once again applying such support to bishops and other ministers (2.26.1–2). The author states specifically that the previous instructions for the ancient prophets are now applicable to the church itself (Connolly 1923, 152). One thus reads:

What was first spoken, hear now: offerings and tithes, first yield are for the high priest Christ and your ministers. . . . Then were first-fruits and tithes and offerings and gifts, but now oblations are offered through the bishop to the Lord God for remission of sin—for they are your high priests.

Quae primum dicta sunt, tu nunc audi: delibationes et decumae primitiva sunt principi sacerdotum Christo et ministris eius . . . quae tunc fuerunt primitvae et decumae et delibationes et dona, nunc sunt prosforae quae per episcopos offeruntur domino Deo in remissione peccatorum—isti enim primi sacerdotes vestri.

14.1 There are similarities and differences between H and ApCon here that suggest a common tradition with variations. H reads as follows:

When you come together on the Lord's day <and> after having acknowledged your offenses so that your sacrifice may be pure, break bread and give thanks.

κατὰ κυριακὴν δὲ κυρίου συναχθέντες κλάσατε ἄρτον καὶ εὐχαριστήσατε προεξομολογησάμενοι τὰ παραπτώματα ὑμῶν, ὅπως καθαρὰ ἡ θυσία ὑμῶν ᾖ

The text of ApCon incorporates much of this same language, though the sentiment is slightly different. ApCon reads as follows (with parallel terminology in italics):

On the day of the resurrection *of the Lord*, called *the Lord's day*, *come together consistently giving thanks* to God and *after having acknowledged* God's mercies on us being rescued through Christ from ignorance, fault, and bondage, *that your sacrifice may be* faultless and acceptable to God

τὴν ἀναστάσιμον τοῦ κυρίου ἡμέραν, τὴν κυριακήν φαμεν, συνέρχεσθε ἀδιαλείπτως, εὐχαριστοῦντες τῷ θεῷ καὶ ἐξομολογούμενοι ἐφ' οἷς εὐηργέτησεν ἡμᾶς ὁ θεὸς διὰ Χριστοῦ ῥυσάμενος ἀγνοίας, πλάνης, δεσμῶν· ὅπως ἄμεμπτος ᾖ ἡ θυσία ὑμῶν καὶ εὐανάφορος θεῷ

ApCon contains additional elements, such as an explicit definition for the "Lord's day" (=Easter?) under the rubric of "day of the resurrection," as well as a soteriological comment on "rescued through Christ" according to "God's mercies," a concept that is not otherwise found within the overt theology of the *Didache*. The reference to "Lord's day," while unusual in early Christian literature otherwise, has rough parallels elsewhere, as with Acts 1:10, Rev 1:10, Ign-Mag 9.1, and Pet 35 and 50 (Rordorf 1968, 212–13; Wengst 1984, 87 n. 116; Jefford 1995, 347–49). Its distinctive usage here, however, makes it clear that ApCon has the *Didache* in mind as a source text for the construction of the narrative. Cf. Draper 2008.

15.1 *So appoint bishops and deacons for yourselves who are worthy of the Lord*: The combination of bishops and deacons alone is unexpected here, since this reference finds parallel only in Paul's opening address at Phil 1:1 and in 1 Clem 42.4–5. Scholars often argue that the Didachist envisions "bishops" (ἐπίσκοποι) to designate a college of bishops and presbyters together (perhaps as with 1 *Clement*). But writing from a later vantage point, ApCon makes a clear distinction between the two positions by the very inclusion of presbyters, an office that the Didachist never actually mentions and thus may not know as authoritative within the community (cf. Jefford 1989, 122–28). ApCon likely writes under the influence of a triple-hierarchy of offices first clearly identified by Ignatius (IgnMag 2; 6.1; IgnTr 2.1–3; 7.2; IgPhd 10.2; IgnSm 8.1) over two centuries earlier. One notes further that the distinction includes an elevation of the role of bishop against that of presbyter and deacon.

15.3–4 *And do not correct one another in anger but in peace, as you have in the gospel*: Once again, the only witness against the reading of H here is provided by ApCon, which does not contain the reference to "as you have in the gospel," making this phrase highly suspect as an editorial insertion into the manuscript tradition by a later hand. The phrase that follows about "let no one speak <to them> nor let <them> hear from you until they repent" also is not paralleled in ApCon, and thus too probably has been added based on Paul's teaching not to associate with those who continue in evil ways, as found in 1 Cor 5:11.

A similar situation arises with 15.4, where one reads in H: "And offer your prayers and charity and all your actions just as you discern in the gospel of our Lord." There is a symmetry in this verse that provides a couplet effect with 15.3, reflecting the concerns of the institutional church in its development (Audet 1958, 467–68). ApCon once again omits this comment, which likely is a general reference to Matt 6:1–18. But the parallel in ApCon contains a comparable instruction: "Observe all things that are commanded you by the Lord." This suggests that while the phrasing in H of "in the gospel of our Lord" here too is likely secondary to the text, some wording that called on the authority "of the Lord" originally stood in this position. Otherwise, there is no evidence to know what this terminology may have been.

16.1 There is some similarity of wording between H and ApCon, though the differences are clear. H reads as follows (provided word-for-word to indicate parallels with ApCon below):
Do not let your lamps go out and be caught unprepared, but be ready. For you do not know the hour in which our Lord comes

οἱ λύχνοι ὑμῶν μὴ σβεσθήτωσαν, καὶ αἱ ὀσφύες <ὑμῶν> μὴ ἐκλυέσθωσαν, ἀλλὰ γίνεσθε ἕτοιμοι· οὐ γὰρ οἴδατε τὴν ὥραν, ἐν ᾗ ὁ κύριος ἡμῶν ἔρχεται

The text of ApCon incorporates some of this same language, yet provides a more complete vision of what the Didachist intends through related imagery. ApCon reads as follows (with parallel terminology in italics):
Let *your loins* be guarded around *and the lamps* burning, and you yourselves be like people who wait for their Lord whenever he might come, in the evening, or morning, or at cock crow, or midnight. *For the Lord will come at an hour they do not expect.*

ἔστωσαν αἱ ὀσφύες ὑμῶν περιεζωσμέναι καὶ οἱ λύχνοι καιόμενοι, καὶ ὑμεῖς ὅμοιοι ἀνθρώποις προσδεχομένοις τὸν κύριον ἑαυτῶν, πότε ἥξει, ἑσπέρας ἢ πρωὶ ἢ ἀλεκτοροφωνίας ἢ μεσονυκτίου· ἢ γὰρ ὥρᾳ οὐ προσδοκῶσιν, ἐλεύσεται ὁ κύριος

It is clear that ApCon has been greatly shaped around the sentiment of Matt 24:50 and Luke 12:35–37, 46, further revealing the author's consideration of the priority of scripture over the words of the *Didache* as authoritative sources.

16.4–5a ApCon diverges from H here, choosing to follow the wording of 2 Thess 2:8–9. The text of H reads as follows:
And then the deceiver of the world will appear as a son of God and perform signs and wonders, and the earth will be handed over into his hands, and he will do such atrocities as have never existed before. Then all humanity will come to the fire of testing, and many will fall away.

ApCon reads alternatively as follows:
And then the deceiver of the world will appear—the enemy of truth, the prince of lies, "whom the Lord Jesus will destroy by the spirit of his mouth," who destroys the ungodly with his lips—and many will fall away.

It is unclear why ApCon selected the imagery of 2 Thessalonians over the wording provided by the Didachist at this point. The *Didache* likewise contains allusions to a variety of scriptural texts, including Matt 24:10, 24; Joel 2:2; 1 Cor 3:13; 1 Pet 1:7; and Zech 13:8–9. It is possible that the author either no longer understood the focus of the Didachist's argument (Milavec 1995, 131–55) or, instead, wished to approach the topic from another perspective. Cf. Draper 1993.

16.5 *By the cursed one himself:* This is a very difficult phrase and may be translated several different ways, such as "by the curse itself" or "through the curse itself." ApCon either has chosen not to include it here, perhaps because of the ambiguity of the phrase's meaning, or because it was not originally part of the source text that the author used. In the current context there is reason to link the phrase with the idea of "fire of testing" that appears earlier in the verse (cf. HermVis 4.3.3–4). But this is not necessarily the intention behind the use of the phrase, and thus the idea of salvation by the "cursed one" (=Christ) is preferred in the translation here (Pardee 1995, 156–76).

16.6–8 This entire closing segment makes a sudden turn toward Matthean materials both in terms of theme and phraseology. While such a conclusion is perhaps not unexpected in the light of other Matthean parallels that run throughout the *Didache*, the focused nature of such equivalents here makes these closing verses particularly intriguing (Kloppenborg 1979, 54–67). Whether one may thus safely assume that this passage originally served as the end of the document remains for scholarly debate.

16.7 *Yet not of all, but as it has been said:* Three passages from scripture are the possible intended reference here (cf. Zech 14:5; Matt 25:31; 1 Thess 3:13), with that of Zechariah being the most likely option (Gordon 1974, 285–89). Once again ApCon has either chosen *not* to incorporate a direct reference to a specific teaching of scripture or has not found it in the author's source text. The theology is highly suspect in H here, indicated by the author's discomfort that a reader might misunderstand that *all* people will be raised at the appearance of the signs (16.6) rather than the righteous alone. It is unclear why ApCon would not share this same concern, unless the wording represents a later correction to the text by a secondary editor of H. This is the more likely scenario.

16.8 It remains unclear whether "on the clouds of the sky" is the end of the *Vorlage* of the *Didache* or, instead, whether some other wording originally followed before its omission by H. Alternative extensions of the text are supported by several literary witnesses, including ApCon, Geor, and the *De abrenuntiatione in baptismate* of Boniface (Aldridge 1999, 1–15). A good case may be made from these optional conclusions that the *Didache* itself once possessed some wording that no longer exists in manuscript form (Audet 1958, 73–74; Wengst 1984, 20; Garrow 2004, 44–66). Nevertheless, the difficulties inherent in any attempt to postulate what that conclusion may have been is only complicated by the limited options that are available from the literary evidence.

BIBLIOGRAPHY

TEXTS AND TRANSLATIONS

Audet, Jean-Paul. 1958. *La Didachè: Instructions des apôtres* (Paris: Gabalda).

Bryennios, Philotheos. 1883. Διδαχὴ τῶν δώδεκα ἀποστόλων ἐκ τοῦ ἱεροσολυμιτικοῦ χειρογράφου νῦν πρῶτον ἐκδιδομένη μετὰ προλεγομένων καὶ σημειώσεων ἐν οἷς καὶ τῆς Συνόψεως τῆς II. Δ., τῆς ὑπὸ Ἰωάνν. τοῦ Χρυσοστόμου, σύγκρισις καὶ μέρος ἀνέκδοτον ἀπὸ τοῦ αὐτοῦ χειρογράφου. Constantinople: Voutyra.

Cody, Aelred. 1995. "The *Didache*: An English Translation." Pp. 3–14 in *The* Didache *in Context: Essays on Its Text, History, and Transmission*. Ed. Clayton N. Jefford. Supplements to Novum Testamentum 77. Leiden: Brill.

Ehrman, Bart D., ed. and trans. 2003. *The Apostolic Fathers*. Pp. 403–43 in the Loeb Classical Library 24–25. Vol 1. Cambridge, Mass. and London: Harvard University.

Funk, F. X. 1905. *Didascalia et Constitutiones apostolorum*. Vol. 1. Paderborn: Schoeningh.

Giet, Stanislas. 1970. *L'énigma de la Didachè*. Publications de la faculté des lettres de l'université de Strasbourg 149. Paris: Ophrys.

Glimm, Francis X., trans. 1947. "The Didache or Teaching of the Twelve Apostles." Pp. 165–84 in Francis X. Glimm, Joseph Marique, and Gerald G. Walsh, trans. *The Apostolic Fathers*. The Fathers of the Church. Vol. 1. Washington: The Catholic University of America.

Goodspeed, Edgar J. 1950. *The Apostolic Fathers: An American Translation*. New York: Harper & Brothers.

Grenfell, Bernard P., and Arthur S. Hunt. 1922. *The Oxyrhynchus Papyri: Part XV*. London: Egypt Exploration Society.

Harris, J. Rendel. 1887. *The Teaching of the Twelve Apostles (ΔΙΔΑΧΗ ΤΩΝ ΑΠΟΣΤΟΛΩΝ): Newly Edited, with Facsimile Text and a Commentary*. London: Clay and Sons; Baltimore: Johns Hopkins University.

Hilgenfeld, Adolf. 1884. *Novum Testamentum extra canonem receptum*. Vol. 4. 2d ed. *Evangeliorum*. Leipzig: Weigel.

Holmes, Michael W. 2007. *The Apostolic Fathers: Greek Texts and English Translations*. 3d ed. Grand Rapids: Baker.

Horner, George W. 1924. "A New Papyrus Fragment of the *Didaché* in Coptic." *Journal of Theological Studies* 25: 225–31.

———. 1904. *The Statutes of the Apostles or Canones Ecclesiastici*. London: Williams & Norgate.

Jones, F. Stanley, and Paul A. Mirecki. 1995. "Considerations on the Coptic Papyrus of the *Didache* (British Library Oriental Manuscript 9271)." Pp. 47–87 in *The* Didache *in Context: Essays on Its Text, History, and Transmission*. Ed. Clayton N. Jefford. Supplements to Novum Testamentum 77. Leiden: Brill.

Kleist, James A., trans. 1948. *The Didache, the Epistle of Barnabas, the Epistles and the Martyrdom of St. Polycarp, the Fragments of Papias, the Epistle to Diognetus.* Ancient Christian Writers. Vol. 6. Westminster, Md.: Newman.

Knopf, D. Rudolf. 1920. *Die Apostolischen Väter.* Vol. 1. *Die Lehre der Zwölf Apostel; Die Zwei Clemensbriefe.* Handbuch zum Neuen Testamentum. Tübingen: Mohr [Siebeck].

Kraft, Robert A., trans. 1978. "The Teaching of the Lord to the Gentiles by the Twelve Apostles (The Didache)." Pp. 303–19 in *The Apostolic Fathers.* Ed. Jack N. Sparks. Nashville: Nelson.

Lake, Kirsopp. 1912. *The Apostolic Fathers.* Pp. 305–33 in The Loeb Classical Library 24–25. Vol. 1. Cambridge, Mass., and London: Heinemann (reprinted 1977).

Lefort, L.-Th. 1952. *Les Pères apostoliques en copte.* Corpus scriptorium christianorum orientalium 135. Scriptores coptici 17. Louvain: Durbecq.

Lightfoot, J. B. 1889–90. *The Apostolic Fathers: Revised Texts with Introductions, Notes, Dissertations and Translations.* 2 parts in 5 vols. London and New York: Macmillan (reprinted Grand Rapids: Baker, 1981).

Lindemann, Andreas, and Henning Paulsen, trans. and eds. 1992. *Die Apostolischen Väter: Griechisch-deutsche Parallelausgabe auf der Grundlage der Ausgaben von Franz Xaver Funk/ Karl Bihlmeyer und Molly Whittaker.* Tübingen: Mohr [Siebeck].

Milavec, Aaron. 2003. *The Didache: Faith, Hope & Life of the Earliest Christian Communities, 50–70 C.E.* New York and Mahway, N.J.: Newman.

Palmer, David Robert. 2011. "ΔΙΔΑΧΗ ΤΩΝ ΑΠΟΣΤΟΛΩΝ—The Teaching of the Apostles: A Critical Greek Edition with footnotes covering textual variants." Online: http://bible-translation.ws/trans/didache.pdf.

Peradse, Gregor. 1932. "Die 'Lehre der zwölf apostel' in der georgischen Überlieferung." *Zeitschrift für neutestamentliche Wissenschaft* 31: 111–16.

Refoulé, Fr., trans. 1990. "La Didachè: Doctrine du seigneur transmise aux nations par les douze apôtres." Pp. 41–64 in *Les écrits des Pères apostoliques.* Intro. Dominique Bertrand. Sagesses chrétiennes; Paris: Cerf (reprinted 2001).

Roberts, Alexander, and James Donaldson, eds. 1867–73. *The Ante-Nicene Fathers: Translations of the Writings of the Fathers down to A.D. 325.* Pp. 369–83 in Vol. 7 (*Lactantius, Venantius, Asterius, Victorinus, Dionysius, Apostolic Teaching and Constitutions, Homily, and Liturgies*). Rev. A. Cleveland Coxe. Edinburgh: Clark (reprinted Grand Rapids: Eerdmans, 1989).

Rordorf, Willy, and André Tuilier. 1978. *La doctrine des douze apôtres (Didachè).* Sources chrétiennes 248 bis. 2d ed. Paris: Cerf (reprinted 1998).

Schaff, Philip. 1885. *The Oldest Church Manual called the Teaching of the Twelve Apostles* (ΔΙΔΑΧΗ ΤΩΝ ΔΩΔΕΚΑ ΑΠΟΣΤΟΛΩΝ): *The Didache and Kindred Documents in the Original with Translations and Discussions of Post-Apostolic Teaching, Baptism, Worship, and Discipline, and with Illustrations and Facsimiles of the Jerusalem Manuscript.* London: Clark.

Schmidt, Carl. 1925. "Das koptische Didache-Fragment des British Museum." *Zeitschrift für neutestamentliche Wissenschaft* 24: 81–99.

Schöllgen, Georg, and Wilhelm Geerlings. 1991. *Didache (Zwölf-Apostel-Lehre); Traditio apostolica (Apostolische Überlieferung).* Vol. 1. Fontes christiani. Freiburg et al.: Herder.

Wengst, Klaus. 1984. *Schriften des Urchristentums: Didache (Apostellehre), Barnabasbrief, Zweiter Klemensbrief, Schrift an Diognet.* Munich: Kösel.

STUDIES AND OTHER
WORKS CITED

Adam, Alfred. 1957. "Erwägungen zur Herkunft der Didache." *Zeitschrift für Kirchengeschichte* 68: 1–47.

Aldridge, Robert E. 1999. "The Lost Ending of the *Didache.*" *Vigiliae Christianae* 53: 1–15.

Balabanski, Vicky. 1997. *Eschatology in the Making: Mark, Matthew and the Didache.* Society for New Testament Studies Monograph Series 97. Cambridge: Cambridge University.

Connolly, R. H. 1923. "The use of the *Didache* in the *Didascalia.*" *Journal of Theological Studies* 24: 145–57.

Draper, Jonathan A. 1992. "Christian Self-definition against the 'Hypocrites' in *Didache* VIII." Pp. 362–77 in *Society of Biblical Literature: 1992 Seminar Papers (No. 31, 128th Annual Meeting, San Francisco, November 21–24, 1992).* Ed. E. H. Lovering. Atlanta: Scholars Press.

———. 2003. "A Continuing Enigma: The 'Yoke of the Lord' in Didache 6.2–3 and Early Jewish Christian Relations." Pp. 106–23 in *The Image of the Judaeo-Christians in Ancient Jewish and Christian Literature.* Ed. Peter J. Tomson and Doris Lambers-Petry. Wissenschaftliche Untersuchungen zum Neuen Testament[1] 158. Tübingen: Mohr Siebeck.

———. 1993. "The Development of the 'Sign of the Son of Man' in the Jesus Tradition." *New Testament Studies* 39: 1–21.

———. ed. 1996. *The* Didache *in Modern Research.* Arbeiten zur Geschichte des Antiken Judentums und des Urchristentums 37. Leiden: Brill.

———. 2011. "Eschatology in the Didache," Pp. 567–82 in *Eschatology of the New Testament and Some Related Documents.* Ed. Jan G. van der Watt. Wissenschaftliche Untersuchungen zum Neuen Testament[2] 315. Tübingen: Mohr Siebeck.

———. 2005. "First Fruits and the Support of Prophets, Teachers and the Poor in Didache 13 in Relation to New Testament Parallels." Pp. 223–43 in *Trajectories through the New Testament and the Apostolic Fathers.* Ed. Andrew Gregory and Christopher Tuckett. Oxford: Oxford University.

———. 2008. "Pure Sacrifice in Didache 14 as Christian Halakah." *Neotestamentica* 42: 223–52.

Drews, Paul. 1904. "Untersuchungen zur Didache." *Zeitschrift für neutestamentliche Wissenschaft* 5: 53–79.

Garrow, Alan J. P. 2004. *The Gospel of Matthew's Dependence on the* Didache. Journal for the Study of the New Testament Supplement Series 254. London and New York: Clark.

Gero, Stephen. 1977. "The So-called Ointment Prayer in the Coptic Version of the Didache." *Harvard Theological Review* 70: 67–84.

Glover, Richard. 1958. "The 'Didache's' Quotations and the Synoptic Gospels." *New Testament Studies* 5: 12–29.

Gordon, Robert P. 1974. "Targumic Parallels to Acts XIII 18 and Didache XIV 3." *Novum Testamentum* 16: 285–89.

Harnack, Adolf. 1886. *Die Apostellehre und die jüdischen Beiden Wege.* Leipzig: Heinrichs'sche Buchhandlung.

———. 1884. *Lehre der zwölf Apostel nebst Untersuchungen zur ältesten Geschichte der Kirchenverfassung und des Kirchenrechts.* Texte und Untersuchungen zur Geschichte der altchristlichen Literatur[2] 1–2. Leipzig: Hinrichs'sche Buchhandlung (reprinted 1893).

Hitchcock, Roswell D., and Francis Brown. 1885. *The Teaching of the Twelve Apostles*. London: Nimmo.

Iselin, L. E. 1895. *Eine bisher unbekannte Version des ersten Teiles der "Apostellehre."* Texte und Untersuchungen zur Geschichte der altchristlichen Literatur[13] 1b. Leipzig: Heusler.

Jefford, Clayton N. 1989. *The Sayings of Jesus in the Teaching of the Twelve Apostles*. Supplements to Vigiliae Christianae 11. Leiden: Brill.

———. ed. 1995. *The* Didache *in Context: Essays on Its Text, History, and Transmission*. Supplements to Novum Testamentum 77. Leiden: Brill.

———. 1997. "Household Codes and Conflict in the Early Church." *Studia Patristica* 31: 121–27.

———. 1989. "Presbyters in the Community of the *Didache*." *Studia Patristica* 21: 122–28.

———. 2010. "Prophecy and Prophetism in the Apostolic Fathers." Pp. 295–316 in *Prophets and Prophetism in Jewish and Early Christian Literature*. Ed. Joseph Verheyden, Korinna Zamfir, and Tobias Nicklas. Wissenschaftliche Untersuchungen zum Neuen Testament[2] 286. Tübingen: Mohr Siebeck.

———. and Stephen J. Patterson. 1989–90. "A Note on *Didache* 12.2a (Coptic)." *The Second Century* 7: 65–75.

Kamlah, Ehrhard. 1964. *Die Form der katalogischen Paränese im Neuen Testament*. Wissenschaftliche Untersuchungen zum Neuen Testament 7. Tübingen: Mohr [Siebeck].

Klinghardt, Matthias. 1996. *Gemeinschaftsmahl und Mahlgemeinschaft: Soziologie und Liturgie frühchristlicher Mahlfeiern*. Texte und Arbeiten zum neutestamentlichen Zeitalter 13. Tübingen & Basel: Francke.

Kloppenborg, John S. 1979. "Didache 16 6–8 and Special Matthean Tradition." *Zeitschrift für die Neutestamentliche Wissenschaft* 70: 54–67.

Köster, Helmut. 1957. *Synoptische Überlieferung bei den Apostolischen Vätern*. Texte und Untersuchungen zur Geschichte der altchristlichen Literatur 65. Berlin: Akademie-Verlag.

LaVerdiere, Eugene. 1996. *The Eucharist in the New Testament and the Early Church*. Collegeville, Minn.: Liturgical Press.

Layton, Bentley. 1968. "The Sources, Date and Transmission of *Didache* 1.3b–2.1." *Harvard Theological Review* 61: 343–83.

McDonald, James I. H. 1980. *Kerygma and Didache: The Articulation and Structure of the Earliest Christian Message*. Society for New Testament Studies Monograph Series 37. Cambridge: Cambridge University Press.

Masseux, Édouard. 1950. *Influence de l'Évangile de saint Matthieu sur la literature chrétienne avant saint Irénée*. Universitas Catholica Lovaniensis[2] 42. Louvain & Gembloux: Louvain University.

Mendelssohn, L. 1890. "Zu den Oracula Sibyllina." *Philologus* 49: 240–70.

Milavec, Aaron. 1995. "The Saving Efficacy of the Burning Process in *Didache* 16.5." Pp. 131–55 in *The* Didache *in Context: Essays on Its Text, History and Transmission*. Ed. Clayton N. Jefford. Supplements to Novum Testamentum 77. Leiden, New York, and Cologne: Brill.

Mueller, Joseph G. 2007. "The Ancient Church Order Literature: Genre or Tradition?" *Journal of Early Christian Studies* 15: 337–80.

Neymeyr, U. 1989. *Die christlichen Lehrer im zweiten Jahrhundert: Ihre Lehrtätigkeit, ihr Selbstverständnis und ihre Geschichte*. Supplements to Vigiliae Christianae 4. Leiden: Brill.

Niederwimmer, Kurt. 1998. *The Didache: A Commentary*. Trans. Linda M. Maloney. Herme-
neia. Minneapolis: Fortress=1st German ed. Göttingen: Vandenhoeck & Ruprecht,
1989.

Pardee, Nancy. 1995. "The Curse that Saves (*Didache* 16.5)." Pp. 156–76 in *The* Didache *in
Context: Essays on Its Text, History and Transmission*. Ed. Clayton N. Jefford. Supplements
to Novum Testamentum 77. Leiden, New York, and Cologne: Brill.

———. 2012. *The Genre and Development of the* Didache: *A Text-Linguistic Analysis*. Wissenschaftliche Untersuchungen zum Neuen Testament[2] 339. Tübingen: Mohr Siebeck.

Peterson, Erik. 1959. "Über einige Probleme der Didache-Überlieferung." Pp. 146–82 in
Frühkirche, Judentum und Gnosis: Studien und Untersuchungen. Rome, Freiburg, and Vi-
enna: Herder.

Robinson, J. Armitage. 1920. *Barnabas, Hermas, and the Didache*. London: SPCK.

Rordorf, Willy. 1981. "Le problem de la transmission textuelle de *Didachè* 1,3b–2,1." Pp. 499–
513 in *Überlieferungsgeschichtliche Untersuchungen*. Ed. Franz Paschke. Texte und
Untersuchungen zur Geschichte der altchristlichen Literatur 125. Berlin: Akademie-
Verlag.

———. 1968. *Sunday: The History of the Day of Rest and Worship in the Earliest Centuries of the
Christian Church*. Trans. A. A. K. Graham. London: SCM.

Sabatier, Paul. 1885. ΔΙΔΑΧΗ ΤΩΝ ΙΒ' ΑΠΟΣΤΟΛΩΝ: *La Didachè ou l'enseignement des douze
apôtres*. Paris: Noblet.

Schaff, Philip. 1885. *The Oldest Church Manual Called the Teaching of the Twelve Apostles*. Edinburgh: Clark.

Schwiebert, Jonathan. 2008. *Knowledge and the Coming Kingdom: The Didache's Meal Ritual and
its Place in Early Christianity*. Library of New Testament Studies 373. New York: Clark.

Stewart(-Sykes), Alistair. 2011. *On the Two Ways: Life or Death, Light or Darkness: Foundational
Texts in the Tradition*. Yonkers, N.Y.: St. Vladimir's Seminary.

Suggs, M. Jack. 1972. "The Christian Two Ways Tradition: Its Antiquity, Form, and Function." Pp. 60–74 in *Studies in New Testament and Early Christian Literature: Essays in Honor
of Allen P. Wikgren*. Ed. David Edward Aune. Supplements to Novum Testamentum 33.
Leiden: Brill.

Taylor, Charles, ed. 1897. *Sayings of the Jewish Fathers comprising Pirqe Aboth in Hebrew and
English with Notes and Excursuses*. 2d ed. The Library of Jewish Classics; Cambridge:
Cambridge University (reprinted N.Y.: KTAV, 1969).

———. 1886. *The Teaching of the Twelve Apostles*. Cambridge: Deighton Bell; London: George
Bell & Sons.

Van de Sandt, Huub, and David Flusser. 2002. *The Didache: Its Jewish Sources and its Place in
Early Judaism and Christianity*. Compendia Rerum Iudaicarum ad Novum Testamentum[3]
5. Assen: Van Gorcum; Minneapolis: Fortress.

Varner, William. 2005. "The Didache's Use of the Old and New Testaments." *The Master's
Seminary Journal* 16: 127–51.

Vokes, F. E. 1938. *The Riddle of the Didache: Fact or Fiction, Heresy or Catholicism?* London: SPCK;
New York: Macmillan.

Vööbus, Arthur. 1968. *Liturgical Traditions in the Didache*. Stockholm: ETSE.

INDEX OF TEXTUAL PARALLELS[*]

OLD TESTAMENT

[*]References are to the notes, indicated by the chapter and verse numbers in the translation. References marked with a dagger (†) are in the Additional Notes found after the translation.

CLASSICAL AUTHORS

ABOUT THE AUTHOR

Clayton Jefford is Professor of Scripture at Saint Mein-
rad Seminary & School of Theology. He holds a Ph.D. from
The Claremont Graduate School (1988) and is the author
of *The Sayings of Jesus in the Teaching of the Twelve Apostles*
(Supplements to Vigilae Christianae, 1997), *Reading the
Apostolic Fathers: A Student's Introduction* (2d edition, 2012),
The Apostolic Fathers and the New Testament (2006), and
most recently, *The Epistle to Diognetus (with the Fragment of
Quadratus)* (2013). He also is the co-editor of the academic
journal *Forum.*